Pippa's Journey

Tail-Wagging Tales of Rescue Dogs

by
Robert U. Montgomery

Praise for Robert Montgomery's Work

"Could not put it down from first opening the cover. It jogged my grey matter and brought back long forgotten fun memories and emotions of growing up in mid- America. It had me laughing out loud throughout! It made me ponder old feelings and brought back precious memories."

—Amazon review of *Under the Bed*

"This book was amazing—perfect summer reading for adults and kids alike! I read it first and enjoyed it and then we read it as a family at bedtime with our 7-year-old, taking turns reading chapters. His favorite chapter was about the toads escaping and he is still giggling about some of the other stories too."

—Amazon review of *Fish, Frogs, and Fireflies*

"The book reminds us to value each moment of our lives, and that time spent fishing is time well spent. Thank you, Mr. Montgomery, for sharing the wonderful journey of your fishing adventures as well as bringing a sweet smile in remembrance of our own."

—Amazon review of *Why We Fish*

NorLightsPress.com
762 State Road 458
Bedford IN 47421

Printed in the United States of America
ISBN: 978-0-9976834-5-5

Book Design by Sammie and Vorris Dee Justesen
Interior by Praditha Kahatapitiya

First printing, 2017

Dedication

This book is dedicated to man's best friend and no-kill animal shelters. A portion of the profit from the sale of each book will be donated to the Farmington Pet Adoption Center, where I found Pippa in 2013.

Table of Contents

Introduction

"We are alone, absolutely alone on this chance planet; and amid all the forms of life that surround us, not one, excepting the dog has made an alliance with us."

—Max DePree

Dogs are not only our best friends—they were our first friends. We domesticated dogs, they domesticated us, or possibly it just happened as wolves scavenged carcasses left by human hunters and loitered around campfires, growing tamer with each generation.

Did it happen 10,000 years ago or 30,000? Scientists aren't certain, just as they aren't sure how and why it all came about. But we do know the relationship was mutually beneficial and has only grown stronger over the centuries. That's evidenced by the estimated 80 million dogs in this country and more than 500 million worldwide.

Eleven dogs have enriched my life, and I can't recall my childhood without visualizing the canines in my life during those formative years. In one of my earliest memories, Chubby, a large mixed breed dog, is planting a sloppy, wet kiss on my face. I could have been as young as two and certainly was no older than three years old.

Squeaky, a small dog reputed to be a chow-rat terrier mix, shadowed me when I first started fishing and exploring the outdoors on my own at age nine or ten. She barked enthusiastically at the bullheads and bluegills I caught and sniffed out most of the turtles I carried home, much to my mother's chagrin. As Squeaky lay near the curb in front of our house, she was killed by a car one summer night. I cried for days.

Happy, a floppy-eared mutt who seemed to wear a perpetual smile, slept at the foot of my bed when I was a teen. My enterprising mother employed her to get me out of bed in the morning: She opened the door and tossed in the cat. Rex, a collie, marched with the local high school band when it practiced across the street and insisted on walking between a girlfriend and me when I brought her home from college.

I could go on and on about the integral part dogs played in my life when I was a child. What makes me sad is that, while I loved them, I never viewed those dogs as anything more than pets.

That perception persisted when I was an adult. Following college and the Army, I lived a nomadic existence for about 15 years, traveling the world, living in apartments, and changing jobs often. As much as I loved dogs, at least I had the good sense to recognize that owning one during that time wasn't a good idea.

Finally I settled in a rural area with a great teaching job and bought my first house. Thinking the time was finally right, I acquired my first dog since being out on my own. She was a malamute pup and I decided to call her Cabal, the name of King Arthur's dog.

The time might have been right, but the breed was a factor I didn't even consider. I wasn't thinking about a dog as a companion. I just wanted a pet. Friendly with people, Cabal grew to be a large, rambunctious dog who preferred being outdoors, even in the coldest weather, and loved roaming the surrounding woods. That was a good fit. But I was away from home from 7 a.m. to 4 p.m. five days a week, while she stayed home alone. Worried about the havoc Cabal might create in my small house if she got bored, I kept her chained in the backyard. I tried leaving her free without supervision, but she always took off and I had to track her down.

We lived that way for seven years, taking long walks together and swimming in nearby lakes and streams when I was home. Cabal remained tethered in the yard when I was gone. Then I had a job offer I couldn't refuse, but it required moving to a city in a much warmer climate and living in an apartment. I couldn't take her with me. So I didn't.

I've been burdened with the guilt ever since. Yes, I found her a good home. Yes, she would have been miserable in the hot weather, even if I could find a place to live with her. Yes, I was being practical. Still, it haunts me. Suddenly torn away from the person with whom she'd lived all her life, what did Cabal think and feel? Did she mourn? Did she adjust? The friend who took her to her new home told me she did, but that reassurance provided small consolation. I cast her aside as if she were little more than a broken appliance.

In painful hindsight, I've recognized that Cabal and all those dogs of my youth thought more of me than I did of them. They felt a bond. They were my protectors, my companions . . . my best friends. And it didn't matter to them that I didn't appreciate them as much as I should have. They didn't ask for anything except to be with me.

Recently I spoke with a friend about this. He acknowledged that he had been the same way and recognized only later in life, as have I, that dogs can be so much more for us than pets, if only we recognize their potential as companions. Sadly, millions of people don't understand this and many never will. That's all too evident in the thousands of dogs chained or imprisoned in small backyard kennels. It's obvious from the millions of canines taken in by shelters each year, many of them dumped onto the streets as casually as if they were empty fast-food containers.

Especially heartbreaking is the fact that dogs, even when mistreated or abandoned, still bond with their people. Dogs' greatest gift to us is also their greatest weakness in terms of their own survival.

"Dogs that permanently lose their masters, their 'family,' are subject to particularly serious emotional trauma, and the symptoms of this are exactly the same as those of children suffering the same fate," said Vilmos Csanyi, an animal behavior expert who spent a decade studying the relationship between humans and canines.

"A dog that has become a burden and is tossed out of a car and left to its own fate will search for his master for days, will not eat, and suffers visibly."

With Ursa, a stray Lab-mix pup I adopted in 1998, I began to understand that dogs are at their finest and happiest when we treat them as companions instead of just pets. As a consequence, we are better and happier too. I'm not sure how this happened. Call it sudden insight coupled with long-overdue maturity on my part. Certainly Ursa needed no epiphany to consider herself my companion, just as Squeaky and Happy didn't decades before.

What did being a companion mean? Well, it meant she stayed in the house with me and went outside only when I did, or when she wanted to soak up some sun on the deck. We walked together twice a day, every day. She napped by my feet when I read, watched TV, or worked at the computer. She went fishing and camping with me. As I lay in my sleeping bag, she'd often put her head on my chest. When the weather was cool enough to allow her to stay in the car, she went shopping and ran errands with me. And, yes, I talked to her.

When Ursa died, I mourned as deeply for her as I did when my mother passed away four years earlier. That might seem a crass comparison for those who've never acknowledged a dog to be more than a pet. But those who truly love dogs will understand. The depth of grief is not determined by species, but by the intimacy of the relationship.

In dealing with my grief, I waited too long—nearly a year—to adopt Pippa, the amazing dog this book is mostly about.

I went to the Farmington Pet Adoption Center (FPAC), a no-kill shelter in Missouri, with the intent of finding a pup. None were available. So, I decided to take a chance and adopt a two-year-old black mixed breed. What sold me was her sweet and calm disposition in the wake of all the canine bedlam in the kennels around her.

I'm not sure where in the adoption process I learned this, but Pippa had spent all of her life at the shelter, surviving heartworm infection, as well as two bouts with mange. What that meant, I later realized, was that she never got to be a puppy. Pippa had little or no socialization and had never bonded with anyone. She didn't know how to give or receive affection. Dog toys were a mystery and held absolutely no interest. Any abrupt noise or sudden movement frightened her, sometimes into mindless panic.

That is not a criticism of FPAC. With a limited budget that allows for few paid positions, the shelter depends on volunteers for much of the work and it survives financially on donations and proceeds from a resale store. Pippa was well cared for in terms of her basic needs, as are the other cats and dogs. But such a restrictive setting doesn't allow a pup to learn how to play, become accustomed to all the sights and sounds of the outside world, and develop emotional attachments.

By my side, Pippa discovered the outside world and, despite her delayed development, blossomed into an intelligent, playful, loving companion. Incredibly, four years later, she's still learning, evolving, and becoming ever more endearing. Perhaps all dogs are like that when we allow them to be. But Pippa was a blank slate when I first brought her home, having missed the most formative years of a dog's life. Awareness of that has sharpened my focus to note, cherish, and catalogue nearly every step in her remarkable journey.

Also, the love, affection, and devotion she now gives generously to me makes me happy beyond words, as does her infectious enthusiasm for life. As I've told my friends so many times that I'm certain they are tired of hearing it, "She makes me smile every day."

That's not to say getting where we are today was easy. We faced challenges. But for the miraculous intervention of kind strangers that first year, I would have been tormented for the rest of my life by a few seconds of carelessness that seemed destined to end in tragedy.

I hope this inspirational chronicle of Pippa's journey will encourage you to consider adopting an adult dog. At least seven million dogs and cats a year go to shelters, and more than half of those, usually adults, are euthanized. Had Pippa not been fortunate enough to land in a no-kill shelter, she could have been one of those fatalities.

If you decide to adopt an adult dog, I've included a chapter on what you should know. Also, Pippa adds her own thoughts in "Adopting an Adult Human" and reveals her fears in "It's a Loud, Scary World."

In addition, you'll find insights into dog breeds, behavior, senses, training, and why our beloved companions do things that confound us, like sniffing butts and rolling in mysterious matter so foul smelling it would make a skunk nauseous.

Pippa's story is divided into Part I: Give Me Shelter and Part III: My Best Friend. In between you will find Part II: Party Animals.

As with my other books, I asked others to contribute. Part II is where you'll find their feel-good stories about lost, abandoned, and homeless dogs who "rescued" them. Randy Joe Heavin shares the story of his beloved Opry, a Lab pup that he found in a big-city night spot and later risked his life to save. Rich Kern tells how Sherwood, a "red Lab," adopted him while he was on an outing with students at a state park. Blake Muhlenbruck writes about Bear, a Lab/German shepherd mix who helped him endure and triumph over a debilitating work injury. Steve Chaconas relates the story of his "Brown Dog," voted class clown of his obedience class and a canine vagabond until he found just the right companion. Sammie Justesen, meanwhile, reveals what it was like to live with Beau, Amos, and Wolf, "Party Animals."

Also be sure to check out two articles in the Appendix: "Why You Should Adopt," which is self-explanatory, and "All Shelters Aren't the Same." Using the Farmington Pet Adoption Center as an example, the latter reveals how a no-kill shelter operates and how it depends on donations and volunteers to keep its doors open. It also explains the differences among various types of shelters and related organizations.

Finally, I hope you'll also check out my other books from NorLights Press:

Under the Bed: Tales From an Innocent Childhood;
Fish, Frogs, and Fireflies: Growing Up with Nature;
and *Why We Fish: Reel Wisdom From Real Fishermen.*

PART ONE: Give Me Shelter

1. Pippa Is Gone

*A*t the least, Pippa was lost, frightened, and starving. More likely she was dead.

Those thoughts haunted me morning, noon, and night for three days.

She was gone, and everything was my fault.

On a quiet, early July morning, less than five months after I adopted her, Pippa and I walked down to the lake and I freed her from her leash so she could splash about. She loved the water, although she seemed to think it was alive. She'd crawl in on her belly and inevitably, make waves with her nose and front legs. As they began to splash her, she'd retreat and bounce along the shoreline just out of their reach. She loved the game and so did I.

With her wet, black coat glistening in the sun, Pippa shook off the excess water, showering me in the process, and we walked back up toward the road. I was just about to reconnect her leash when the firecracker exploded. In a heartbeat she went from happy-go-lucky to panicked. I saw it for an instant in her brown eyes. And then she bolted.

"Pippa! Pippa! Come here, girl," I called as soothingly as I could. "Come here! Pippa!" Somehow, some way, my voice and/or the sound of her name, bulldozed through the fear that gripped her. She stopped, turned, and slowly, tentatively, started back toward me.

Thank God!

Pippa was within four or five feet, just out of arm's reach, when the second firecracker exploded.

And she was gone, running as fast as she could be to anywhere but there.

For most of three days and two nights I replayed that scenario in my mind, alternating it with another nightmare that occurred about 16 months before, one I thought I'd moved past. Now it returned with a vengeance, for I also felt guilt about what happened with another dog, my beloved Ursa, on her last day of life.

What happened on that day, I realized, probably explained why I waited for nearly a year before adopting Pippa from a no-kill shelter. Intellectually, I had come to realize that I shouldn't beat myself up emotionally about what had occurred on Ursa's final day with me. But the inevitability of life ending for my canine companion who was nearly 14 years old had been compounded by an incident that, however minimal in its actual impact, remained a horrific visual I would never forget.

* * * * *

When Ursa was 10, the vet warned me that "the end can come quickly" for large dogs. A red Lab-Rhodesian ridgeback mix, she weighed about 75 pounds, and over the years, required ligament surgery on both back legs. When she was 12, I started keeping her away from stairs and shortened our morning and evening walks.

In all other ways, though, she remained happy and healthy until a week in late March. Her normally robust appetite waned. She wandered about as if not sure of where she was or where she was going.

As most anyone who loves his dog would, I tried to ignore the symptoms. I rationalized that she just wasn't feeling well and she'd be back to normal soon. The fear that I might end her life prematurely outweighed the reality of what was happening.

By Friday, though, I'd just about made peace with the fact that soon I would need to take her to the vet for a fatal injection. She would no longer eat and had lost too much weight. Walking was difficult. I didn't want her to suffer.

As I stood on the deck at the back of my house, I talked by phone to a friend with more experience at this than I. I thought Ursa was on her bed in the garage at the front of the house. I believed that because she hadn't even bothered to rise and greet me when I returned home about 30 minutes before.

She normally slept in the house, but because I was away and the weather was so nice, I moved her to the garage, under the care of my neighbors for my brief business trip. Suddenly, there she was near the top of the steep flight of steps leading up to the deck. She was one step away from hobbling onto the deck because she wanted to be with me. I'm not sure what happened next. But what I saw is burned painfully and forever into my mind. She raised a front leg and held it for an instant before tipping over backward, possibly because her back legs gave out. Then she plunged down those steps onto the concrete below, her left leg wedged into the side railing.

She didn't whine. She didn't cry out. And I could find no bleeding or broken bones. I freed her leg and we sat there for a while on the concrete. As I stroked her head, she closed her eyes, shielding me from seeing the cataracts that now clouded them, yet another reminder of the brevity of a dog's life in general and, just then, hers in particular. I fought back tears. When I finally judged we both had regained enough strength, I gently led her back to her bed in the garage.

Her breathing was labored as she lay down. Eventually, it evened out a bit and she closed her eyes once again.

I didn't want her to be hurt from her attempt to be with me on what would be her last day of life. Bad enough that she was old and I faced a heart-wrenching decision as to how and when she would die.

I'll never know what, if any damage, the fall did. But a couple of hours later she struggled to her feet and walked out into the yard, where she collapsed. Slowly, she raised her head as she lay in the new green grass of a beautiful spring evening.

For a brief moment, she looked like the pup I brought home so long ago who went tearing through the house with the toilet paper in her mouth on that first day. She looked like the dog who loved to munch ice cubes, who loved to ride in the car, and who never met a child or another dog she didn't like.

But she was dying. I called the after-hours vet who agreed to meet me at her office. My friends helped me place my good old girl on her bed and into the car. And I took her for one last ride.

* * * * *

The vet's reassuring words on Ursa's final day did little to convince me that I hadn't contributed to her death. Over time the guilt lessened and I stopped playing the mental video of her fall on a constant loop. Still, I suspect my psyche had to heal before I felt worthy enough, responsible enough, to have another canine companion.

Finally, in late February, nearly a year later, I adopted Pippa, a two-year-old "Lab mix" who spent the first two years of her life in a shelter. I knew she was easily frightened by thunder, gunshots, and other sudden, concussive noises. I knew she still had much to learn about the world in general, and then adjust to it. And I knew I should be especially careful on that July 4th weekend. Still, I never suspected someone would set off firecrackers at 7:30 a.m. on an otherwise peaceful morning in a rural area.

I was wrong.

And just as horrific as the sight of Ursa falling down those steps was what I feared would be my last vision of Pippa, ears back, running as fast as she could toward . . . what? Starving to death? Being shot by an angry farmer or hit by a car?

"Pippa!Pippa!" I screamed and chased after her. "Pippa!"

I ran and called and ran until I could no longer see her.

She had spent just a few months in the outside world, with me to show her, teach her, and protect her as she explored and adjusted to a totally alien environment, where water was alive and sounds provoked mindless panic.

And I had failed.

2. Give Me Shelter

"Acquiring a dog may be the only time a person gets to choose a relative."

—*Mordecai Siegal*

*I*wanted a puppy. Who doesn't? They're cute and cuddly and squirm when you hold them, as they try to lick your face.

The dogs of my childhood—Chubby, Squeaky, Lady, Happy, and Rex—were pups when we brought them home. So was Ursa, who had died nearly a year earlier after being my companion for nearly 14 years. She was about three months old when my sister found her wandering around a school yard, covered in ticks.

Of course, I didn't remember the tedious part about bringing puppies into our home when I was a child. My parents, God bless them, took care of most of that, including house breaking and escorting pups through those months when they wanted to chew, chew, chew on shoes, clothes, furniture, and anything else they could sink their teeth into.

Much to my surprise, with Ursa, I quickly realized that raising her to be a well behaved Lab/Rhodesian ridgeback mix really wasn't that difficult. As a teacher, I had found students were better behaved and learned more when I was consistent and followed through on what I promised—or threatened. Ursa was my new pupil and I treated her the same way.

She pooped and peed in the house just a couple of times before she learned the drill. After a brief infatuation with rolls of toilet paper as objects to destroy, she quickly turned her attention to the stuffed animal toys I gave her. At first, she tore and dismembered them, as most any pup would do. But quickly, it seemed, she grew to love them. In fact, she loved them all through her life, and if she saw one, anywhere at any time, she would appropriate it and try to take it home with her.

As an exuberant pup, Ursa also humored me as I taught her to chase, catch, and return a Frisbee. Eventually, though, she decided chasing just wasn't her thing, whether it was toys, balls, or squirrels. If I threw something to her, she'd catch it as proficiently as any baseball outfielder, and she'd bring it to me. But except for long walks in the morning and evening, she preferred the sedentary life, and eating ice cubes or going swimming on hot, summer days. Thunder, fireworks, gun shots—nothing of the sort frightened her. I could vacuum her and she wouldn't stir.

All those pleasant memories of sharing my life with Ursa as she grew from pup to adult and developed a unique personality played no small part in my desire to get another pup.

"I'm sorry," said the woman at the Farmington Pet Adoption Center, a no-kill facility. "We don't have any puppies. But we have some nice adult dogs. Would you like to see them?"

An adult dog? Yikes! Why would I want to take home someone else's problem? Surely most of them must be animals previous owners had decided that they didn't want any longer. Maybe they bit people. Maybe they were hostile to small children or other family pets. Maybe they suffered from anxiety when left alone and tore up everything in sight. Yeah, some of them might be dogs that simply got lost and their owners never found them. But why take the chance when a puppy was a safer—and much cuter—option?

But they had no puppies. And I had driven 25 miles. Couldn't hurt to see what my options were, I decided.

"Okay," I said. "I'll take a look."

*   *   *   *   *

February weather in Missouri is typically cold and often wet, so all of the adult dogs were housed inside in individual cyclone fence kennels, perhaps 10 x 12 feet in size, adjacent to one another. There might have been 15 or 20 dogs, but within seconds, it sounded more like 100.

Our arrival signaled one to start barking and, within seconds, all seemed to join in, with a few ear-piercing howls for variety. My first thought was, "This is the canine equivalent of a psychiatric ward." I didn't want to be there.

However, as I walked past their cages the dogs became individuals instead of one maniacal pack of irrational beasts. Many eagerly came forward, imploring attention and affection. Some backed up and watched intently, as if waiting to react instead of act. A few retreated to the back of their pens and huddled there, still barking or howling.

But what startled me the most, what will stay with me forever, was the universal look in their eyes that spoke of both fear and hope. Almost certainly they were accustomed to seeing volunteer staff, but I was a stranger, and, for good or bad, that signaled something. What I saw in those imploring eyes was "I want to go home with you. Please. Please, take me." And I also saw the fear that I would not. Yes, I'm probably attributing human qualities to canines. But that's what I saw. Every time I go to a shelter now, as I did recently with a friend, that's what I see. And it saddens me beyond words.

Suddenly, my decision was not whether to adopt an adult dog, but which one. And, yes, that was purely an emotional response, probably one volunteer shelter workers hope people will have if they can just get them to look at adult dogs.

Yet, I wasn't entirely brain dead. I realized I must be rational and reasonable in narrowing my choices. Of course, I had no idea what my criteria should be, so maybe I'm just rationalizing now about a decision that was totally emotional.

She was the only dog among the canine cacophony who wasn't barking or howling. Full disclaimer here: As much as I love dogs, I hate barking, especially pointless, neurotic barking. Ask my dog-owner friends; it's a standing joke about me. And for that noisy and needless barking, I blame irresponsible owners more than their dogs. As if to alert me of potential danger, Ursa had barked only when someone came to the door, and then briefly. That required no training on my part either. She was just that way.

A medium-size black dog with white toes and a little white on her chest came meekly to the kennel gate and looked at me with sad, brown eyes. Information posted on the gate said she was two years old, a "Lab mix," and her name was "Barb." Aside from the color of her hair

and her eyes, she didn't look like a Lab mix. With a pointed nose, she was streamlined and built for speed, with a thinner coat than a Lab would have. But her genetic ancestry was irrelevant anyway.

I was attracted to her.

"Would you like to take her for a walk?" the staffer asked. "She's very good on a leash."

And she was, indeed, very good. She didn't pull, jump, or try to escape in any way. She stayed beside me as we walked, and when I stopped, she leaned against my leg. That all but sealed the deal.

Inside, workers told me Barb had been born at the shelter two years before, along with siblings, all of whom had been adopted. In other words, this sweet, docile dog had spent her entire life behind bars, except when taken out briefly for exercise and to go to the bathroom. She obviously was built for running, but probably had never run in her life.

That did seal the deal for me, and I wanted to cry as I thought of how Barb spent her first two years of life. That wasn't the fault of the shelter and the wonderful people who work there. If not for it and them, the dog I had decided to adopt probably would have died. Still, this sleek, beautiful animal had never known what it was like to be free, to run unfettered until exhaustion, and then collapse in the grass to regain her breath with the sweet, fresh air of the outdoors.

"And she's very smart," another worker added, as I filled out the paperwork.

*　　*　　*　　*　　*

By the time I picked her up a few days later, I had decided that Barb would be known from that point on as "Pippa." Honestly, I don't know where that name came from, just as I don't know why

I gave Ursa the name that I did. She just looked like a Pippa to me. And, no, I had no knowledge of a British socialite named Pippa Middleton, whose sister married Prince William in 2011. Yes, I do now because so many people have asked me if there's a connection.

My new companion had been named Barb, I learned, because litter mates were given names with the same first initial to facilitate record keeping. In looking over her health records, I also saw she had suffered two bouts with mange and another with heart worm. She was a survivor.

And just as I was about to leave with my new companion, a shelter staffer told me something that absolutely stunned me and about which I will write more later.

"Black dogs are really hard to find homes for," she said. "They're just like black cats. People don't want them."

Pippa, however, was one black dog who did find a home— with me. I had waited too long after Ursa died to find another companion. And I couldn't wait for our adventure together to begin.

3. Getting to Know You

*I*f Harry Houdini, legendary magician and escape artist, had been standing next to me as I stared at the empty kitchen, I'm confident he would have said, "Wow! How did she do that?"

And, shaking my head in disbelief, I would have answered, "I have no idea."

For her first time at home alone, I could have locked Pippa in her crate, where she slept and which was her safe place. Or I could have closed her in the small laundry room that separated the kitchen from the garage. I quickly ruled out that, however, for it was as small as the kennel at the shelter, where she spent the first two years of her life. It might not have bothered her to be shut in there for a couple of hours. In fact, it probably would have seemed ordinary. But the thought of doing that to her made me sad beyond words.

The unfinished portion of the basement was another option, but I had lots of fishing tackle and gardening equipment down there, and I wasn't yet certain how she would behave when left alone. I didn't want to come home and find her tangled in monofilament line, chewing on the cork handle of a fishing rod, or rolling in smelly compost from a bag she ripped open. I had been spoiled by Ursa's exemplary behavior, but I heard plenty of horror stories of dogs left alone and the havoc they could wreak on clothing, furniture, carpeting, and even walls and doors.

So the kitchen it was. In the two weeks we'd been together, I watched Pippa enough to know she was more athletic than any dog I'd ever seen, except on television. Although she weighed only about 45 pounds, when she reared up while playing, her legs were long enough for her front paws to rest on my shoulders. And with a little training she could give those TV canines a run for their money on agility courses. I cleared off the cabinets to remove temptation. And then I built barricades across the two doorless entries, using folding tables, chairs, Pippa's crate, cardboard boxes, and a portable room divider. The only things missing were rolled barbed wire across the top and guard towers. Builders of the Berlin Wall had nothing on me. I felt confident Pippa wouldn't be going anywhere, despite her athleticism.

I gave her a treat, told her I would be back soon, and left through the laundry room. But later, when I came in the same way, she was gone. Although she was agile and often used her long nose as a tool in much the same way chimpanzees use sticks to dig termites out of a mound, I didn't think she could open two doors into the garage, punch the button to slide open the garage door, and then enter the code on the outside pad to close it.

But I wasn't ruling it out. Not yet anyway. Both barricades were just as I left them, and Pippa wasn't in the kitchen. I called her and received no response. The house was an empty quiet. It felt weirdly ominous and I identified with The Three Bears who came home to learn that someone had been in their porridge. I called again and heard nothing except the refrigerator.

I tore down one of the barricades and went in search of my own Goldilocks. Turning on lights as I progressed, I saw that my office was empty and nothing had been knocked over, chewed on, or otherwise damaged. No doggie porn on the laptop. The guest bathroom was vacant too, as was the guest bedroom.

The living room was another story. Pippa wasn't there, but she had been, leaving a big pile of poop and a puddle of pee just in front of the television set. Perhaps she'd been watching Animal Planet when nature called.

Don't scoff. At this point, I wasn't so sure she couldn't have used her nose to press the "on" button on the remote or the garage door opener. Somehow she had escaped the kitchen without disturbing the barricades. Also, for years I had watched my friend's dog, Daisy, pay rapt attention to the TV, just waiting for any animal that wasn't human, whether a horse in a Western, a lion in a National Geographic special, or a lizard in a commercial. Then she barked incessantly until it was gone. If it was moving right to left, she followed it off the screen and looked for it through the adjacent sliding glass door. Ursa, my companion before Pippa, never understood what all the commotion was about. Maybe Pippa did. And maybe she used her nose to turn off the set when she had finished watching. But where was she now? "Pippa!" I called for the third or fourth time.

Only one room remained, my darkened bedroom at the back of the house. I flipped the switch . . . and there she was, my sleek, black Goldilocks, sprawled gloriously in the middle of my bed. The light awakened her—or perhaps she pretended it did—and she smiled broadly, her long tongue lolling out the side. Yeah, I know it probably wasn't a smile. But it looked like one, as her brown eyes twinkled in the light. This smile provided the first expression of genuine happiness toward me I had seen from Pippa since bringing her home. Until then, she had been docile and passive, except when learning to play outside, accepting affection but not really seeking it either, showing little or no personality.

Suddenly, she had one, and it shone brighter than the overhead light. In that moment, at least, she was a mischievous imp. Despite myself, I couldn't help but smile—and wonder what other surprises lay ahead as Pippa and I became accustomed to one another.

The smile didn't remain as I cleaned up the mess in the living room. No matter how many times I've cleaned up dog poop over the years, it never gets any easier and my gag reflex quickly kicks into high gear. If I had adopted a puppy, I'm certain, I would have been gagging a lot more. Fortunately, Pippa wasn't inclined to relieve herself in the house, even from the beginning. And that was pretty amazing, considering she hadn't been house broken. Instead, she had the option of going on a potty pad in her cage at the shelter.

Immediately, I started her on a routine of walks first thing in the morning and then in late afternoon, and she quickly adapted to going to the bathroom during those times. Most of the time anyway. Along with the living room deposit, her first poop away from the shelter was a notable exception.

When I brought Pippa home, she didn't eat, drink, or go to the bathroom for nearly two full days. When I called the shelter a worker told me such behavior wasn't unusual for a dog in a new environment. She advised me to give Pippa a little more time. Since she seemed healthy in every other way, I relaxed a little and decided to take my new companion to visit my neighbors, Bob and Daisy.

Bob maintained a smorgasbord of doggie treats for his black Lab. His theory was that sometimes his TV-watching dog needed a treat to whet her appetite. When I told him about Pippa's refusal to eat, he said, "Let's try this," as he pulled out chicken jerky, which was Daisy's favorite.

Turns out, it was Pippa's too. She gobbled down a large piece. Bob grinned broadly, as she looked up expectantly for another. That evening, she ate her first meal at home, seeming to confirm Bob's theory.

Pippa, however, didn't save her first poop for home, or even for the walk on our way back home. A few minutes after eating the jerky, she gave back to Bob, so to speak, with a steaming pile on his basement floor.

We still laugh about that to this day. Pippa might be my dog, but she ate her first meal and had her first poop at his house.

---

4. Let's Take a Walk

"Some of our greatest historical and artistic treasures we place with curators in museums; others we take for walks."

— *Roger Caras*

"I'm taking a walk. I'm going outside. I'm watching the birds. I'm just getting by."

That song by John Prine is what finally convinced me I waited too long following Ursa's death to get another canine companion. My friend Skyler included it on an iPod she gave me as a Christmas present. She knew my tastes as well as my habits, and thought it appropriate, I guess. She was right.

Ursa and I walked thousands of miles during our nearly 14 years together. I didn't start our adventures with any kind of idea as to objective or intent. Living in a rural area and loving the outdoors as I do, it just seemed the logical thing to do with my dog. Somewhere along the way, an occasional walk evolved into daily morning and evening excursions of at least a mile and sometimes three or more.

And, yes, I know the benefits of walking daily: maintain healthy weight, strengthen bones and muscles, improve mood, improve balance and coordination, and prevent or manage various conditions, including heart disease, high blood pressure, and type 2 diabetes. Plus, according to the Mayo Clinic, "The faster, farther, and more frequently you walk, the greater the benefits."

Additionally, a recent study from Europe suggests that regular walks can add seven years to your lifespan.

But, honestly, knowledge of long-term health effects wasn't nearly as important as spending time with my best buddy, for whom our walks were the absolute highlight of each day. Seeing her pace eagerly in front of the door as I put on my shoes and then went to the closet for my jacket, made me smile. I loved watching her race outside to sniff grass and trees, splash in the water, mark her territory with an obligatory squirt, and chase the occasional squirrel. Dogs are happier, more responsible, and less destructive companions when you are consistent with their discipline and give them regular activities and rewards to anticipate. That's my opinion anyway.

And so are people. Based on our too short time together, I think Ursa would agree, for I suspect she studied me as much as I studied her. And when she died, I was left to walk alone. For awhile, the iPod seemed to be enough, especially when I played Queen's "We Are the Champions," Warren Zevon's "Lawyers, Guns, and Money," The Mountain Goats' "Up the Wolves," Jerry Jeff Walker's "L.A. Freeway," Little River Band's "Cool Change," and Starship's "We Built This City." Gradually, though, that John Prine song sneaked into my playlist of favorites and I realized songs and daily exercise weren't enough for me: "I'm watching the birds. I'm just getting by."

So, about 11 months after Ursa's final trip to the vet, I adopted Pippa. I took the iPod with me for the first few days of the twice-a-day walks that started immediately. Soon, though, I left it in the kitchen drawer, not just because Pippa needed training and attention, but because the joy she derived from the simplicity of a walk provided ample entertainment and made me immeasurably happy.

*   *   *   *

Ursa and Pippa couldn't have been more different in terms of energy and enthusiasm. Ursa was mellow and laid back from the time she was a pup, when I taught her to chase and catch a Frisbee. Eventually she trained me to throw it directly to her, so she didn't have to chase it. As often as not, she followed me on our walks, instead of leading the way. Conversely, Pippa was high energy and, with her slender build and long legs, made for speed. Possibly two years of confinement in a kennel contributed to her delight in suddenly exploding into blinding bursts for no apparent reason other than she could. Three-mile walks for me translated into six-mile runs for her.

Both dogs were sweet, docile, and great with children and other dogs. Perhaps that's why Pippa quickly perpetuated Ursa's tradition of bringing home lost or abandoned animals from our walks.

Ursa brought three: a mixed breed, a yellow Lab pup, and a husky. I didn't speak to, pet, or offer encouragement to them in any way. They just liked Ursa's looks, I guess. Perhaps she communicated something to them with her brown eyes: "I was lost too. Now I've got a good thing here. Follow me."

As if totally exhausted, the small dog of mixed ancestry plopped down in the yard when we got back home. His posture seemed to say, "Okay, I've had it. Can someone bring me some water, please? And maybe make a phone call for me?"

Fortunately, because he was wearing tags, I was able to do that. The little boy who accompanied his father to my house was overjoyed to get his dog back.

Also, wearing ID tags, the Lab and the husky wanted to join Ursa inside for breakfast. Perhaps she had invited them when I wasn't looking. I secured them in the garage, gave them food and water, and called their owners. Three lost dogs, and three happy endings, courtesy of Ursa.

Pippa wasted little time in following tradition. Within weeks of her adoption, she brought home a Great Pyrenees, a monster of a dog at least four times her svelte 45 pounds.

We passed it lying in the yard of a house being rehabbed by a friend. Because the dog was loose and so large, I was reluctant to get near it at first, especially since it was chewing on a large bone of some sort, possibly a remnant from someone who had the misfortune of getting too close previously. I say that because the bone was relatively fresh, with traces of flesh still attached.

"He's been there all day," my friend reassured me. "He seems friendly enough. He hasn't bothered anyone."

So, without speaking to the dog or acknowledging it in any way, I led Pippa past the massive beast gnawing on what I later learned was a deer bone. Picking up its treasure, the Great Pyrenees arose, as if drawn by a Siren's call or perhaps the hypnotic song of a magical piper, and fell in line behind us. For more than a mile he followed us, all the way back to my house, and then plopped down in the yard to resume chewing.

Finally confident that he posed no threat, I released Pippa from her leash so she could conclude our walk the way that she always does. Only this time, she didn't run laps and roll on her back in the lush spring grass with orgasmic pleasure. Instead she approached her new friend and his bone. Tail wagging, he stood to say hello, and she snatched the treasure.

Uh,oh. Pippa wouldn't have a chance against this brute if he attacked her, I knew. Her only hope would be to drop the bone and run. But would she?

No, she would not. Instead, she dropped into the grass and commenced chewing on her prize. When the Great Pyrenees approached, she growled, a low, barely discernible warning, but loud enough for both the big dog and me to hear it. Immediately, he fell to his belly and crawled toward her in supplication, whining as he did so.

I was stunned. Pippa was unperturbed. "No," she said again via canine communication, and continued merrily gnawing on the bone. Although it was an outlandish theory, I suddenly wondered if Pippa had waited to make her move on the prize until we got home because it was too large for her to carry.

And I saw this as a pivotal moment in our new relationship. Despite her much smaller size, she was the alpha to the Great Pyrenees. Had she accepted me as the alpha in our relationship or would she growl at me if I reached for the bone? I remembered Ursa, sweet, lovable, Ursa, growling at my girlfriend who tried to move her food bowl as she was eating.

I decided to take the chance, and Pippa didn't challenge me. I already was the alpha of our pack, thank goodness. But now I had a deer bone in my hand and two dogs who wanted to chew on it.

I led them into the basement, left our visitor there with his treasure, and took Pippa upstairs for treats. Knowing he was friendly, I took a look at the tags on his collar, made a phone call, and reunited him with his owners, who had recently adopted him from a shelter. He was about five miles from home. I reminded them to take his bone with them.

Shortly thereafter, Pippa went from one extreme to the other. Somewhere on our way back home from a morning walk, three little gray and white kittens fell in line behind us. Now, I tell people about this and often they don't believe me. I don't blame them either. The phrase "like trying to herd cats" comes to mind. But they did, indeed, follow us, even though plenty of houses were around they could have gravitated to, after some reprehensible human being abandoned them.

When they decided to tag along, I don't know. Pippa obviously didn't mind the new additions because she didn't alert me. I noticed, though, when we were at least a half mile from home. That's right: Those little kittens, with no momma and no mittens, elected to follow me and Pippa, who seemed to have become the pied piper of lost pets.

Both incredulous and amused, I decided to see how far I could take this. Instead of stopping at my house, Pippa and I walked another quarter-mile across a lake dam to a friend's house. The kittens followed.

I told my friend what happened and we chatted for awhile. The kittens explored and Pippa watched. Then, halfway hoping the kittens would stay at my friend's house and become his responsibility, I headed back home with Pippa.

Again, the kittens followed. As we walked along the dam, I called the local animal shelter with my cell phone to tell them about the orphans. "Sorry," a male voice said. "We take only dogs."

So . . .back at my house, I took Pippa inside through the walk-in basement, leaving the kittens on the patio. With her fed, I checked to see if the trio had moved on for greener pastures. While I didn't dislike cats, I didn't want one for a pet, not to mention three. Surely, they could find someone, somewhere, to take them in.

They hadn't left. Instead, they were trying in vain to get a drink from the mouth of the garden hose. Seeing that, my fragile resistance cracked. Immediately, I turned on the water and they eagerly lapped at it.

Now what? I certainly didn't have cat food on hand. I gave them milk, put a folded blanket on the concrete for a bed, and went inside to call my contact at Farmington Pet Adoption Center, where I adopted Pippa. She said the no-kill center didn't have room for more cats. But she countered that if I would foster the kittens for awhile, the center would provide food as we tried to find homes for them. I agreed.

Although I didn't want three cats, I felt obliged to help. If Pippa had been in a traditional animal shelter, I wouldn't have found her. She would have been euthanized after only a few weeks or months. Instead, she was in a place staffed by caring people and financed by donations. For two years, they looked out for her, helping her survive both illness and disease.

I picked up the food, and then we placed notices on Facebook and waited for someone to show interest. The kittens, meanwhile, made themselves at home around  my house. They sprawled in flower pots on the front porch, nestled together for naps on the patio, and showed not the slightest inclination to leave.

In a short time, we found homes for them. When people saw them in person, they were just too cute and cuddly to resist. I can describe the kittens that way with confidence because that's how I came to see them as well, despite my resistance early on and attempts to rid myself of them as quickly as possible. If others hadn't taken them, I suspect, Pippa and I would soon have been sharing our beds with them.

Looking back, I suspect that reuniting those dogs with their owners and finding home for the kittens was "paying it forward" for Ursa, Pippa, and me in exchange for our good fortune in finding one another.

Admittedly, though, I am a little nervous thinking about what might follow us home next.

5. Free at Last

"The dog was created especially for children. He is the god of frolic."

—Henry Ward Beecher

*A*fter bringing Pippa home from the shelter, where she spent the human equivalent of her childhood and early teen years, I kept her on a leash for several days as we took morning and evening walks. I also frequently led her around the perimeters of my property to familiarize her with her "territory."

A shelter worker had told me Pippa was "good" on a leash, and she was correct. No straining. No jerking. From the start, Pippa was my perfectly behaved walking buddy. A life lived in confinement no doubt played a part in

that, as did workers who spent time with her when she wasn't in an indoor pen or outdoor kennel.

I wasn't taking notes or recording video, so I can't tell you precisely how many days passed before I allowed her off that leash, nor can I show you what happened when I did. I wish that I could.

But whether it happened on the fourth, fifth, or maybe even the sixth day, that moment will live with me forever. Remembering it fills my heart with happiness and my eyes with tears. For possibly the first time in her life, Pippa, a dog made for running if ever there was one, ran. She ran, and ran, and ran. Remarkably, she didn't go far, possibly because of the time I spent familiarizing her with her new home. Rather, she ran laps in much the same way sprinters circle a track or greyhounds pursue a decoy rabbit.

Ears back, tail down, Pippa was a canine flash, a black blur as she raced around the edges of the yard. Again, and again, and again—until she collapsed in the brown grass of winter, long tongue lolling out the side of her mouth in what appeared to be a beatific smile and brown eyes flashing with delight. Her rapid breathing fogged the cold air. Yeah, I know, I might be anthropomorphizing. We do that often with animals, especially our four-legged companions. But if there were a scale by which to measure happiness in dogs, I assure you, her reading was off the charts.

Mine as well, as I remembered the sweet, but passive and docile dog I brought home just a few days before—an animal who showed little emotion of any kind, or any desire for affection. In other words, until this moment, she seemed just a boarder in my home, an animal I fed and watered and took for walks, but who gave no indication she was happier with me than she had been at the shelter.

This was a breakthrough. Of that I was certain, although I also knew we needed more time for her to recognize me as someone rather than just another human who met her basic needs. How far we had to go, though, and how long it would take, would have saddened me a bit if I had known. However, that knowledge also would have helped me prevent the tragedy that unfolded about four months later.

But just then, on that late February day, all that mattered for us both was Pippa's exuberant exhaustion.

In the days that followed, Pippa and I both added to her afternoon post-walk play time. First, as she circled the yard one afternoon, she suddenly veered off into a border of large shrubs along the edge of my property. And she didn't come out.

As someone well acquainted with a dog's super sensitive sense of smell, I wasn't surprised. Just as the rest of the outside world was new to Pippa, so was the multitude of odors she encountered for the first time. I didn't mind cutting her some slack for periodic pauses and detours to partake of a particularly alluring fragrance on our walks, or during her happy time back at home.. Of course, eventually she bolted back out of the foliage and resumed her laps.

At some point, I made a game of her disappearances into the shrubbery. When she was out of sight, I yelled, "Where's Pippa? Where's Pippa?" And, as if she knew exactly what I was saying, she charged out and ran rings around me until exhausted. As the weather warmed, even the neighbors across the road stopped their yard work to enjoy these theatrics, which she eventually expanded to their property, with my permission.

Also, I found a ball. A Winnie the Pooh ball, to be precise. From the first time I threw it, Pippa loved the ball. She chased it down, and then pranced around with head held high. One time, as she jerked her head up, the ball flew from her mouth and again she ran it down. Perhaps she intended to do that. Perhaps not. But I'd swear on a stack of Bibles that from then on she often intentionally threw the ball so that she could chase it and then do it again.

About this time, the thought occurred to me that teaching her to fetch and bring the ball to me would be easy. She was a natural, and I had taught Ursa, her predecessor, not only to fetch, but to catch balls and Frisbees in midair. I tossed the ball above Pippa's head and she lunged for it. She missed, the ball bouncing high off her nose, exciting her just as much as when she threw it herself. She ran it down and threw it again.

I tried coaxing her to bring the ball to me after I tossed it for her to chase. She would have none of it. She'd come to me, but leave the ball behind, where it stayed until I picked it up and threw it again for her. Yeah, I know. Pippa was teaching me to fetch the ball, instead of the other way around.

Still, I have no doubt I could have reined her in and taught her to be the fetcher instead of the thrower. Just as a shelter worker had told me, Pippa was smart. Although she was dubbed "Barb" at the shelter, she instantly responded to her new name. She picked up routines, as well as basic commands to come, sit, and stay. As quick and agile as she was, I also think I could have taught her to jump through hoops and navigate canine obstacle courses with the best of them.

But she had too much fun playing and being free for the first time in her life. Structuring that play, I decided, would be mostly about me and proving to myself what I could do with this amazing animal. Yeah, I know, dogs have been domesticated and bred for thousands of years to meet our needs. We train them. They live to please. That's the way it works.

I didn't want to do that with Pippa. I didn't want to risk diminishing even in the slightest way the happiness she had too long been deprived of. No matter what I trained her to do, including bring me beer from the refrigerator, it couldn't be better than this, for her or me. As long as she was obedient, nothing else mattered in terms of training, for I could protect her from harm and prevent her from frightening others.

Not that Pippa ever would hurt anyone. Quite the opposite, in fact. Once she learned to accept and enjoy affection from me, she began to seek it out from others, including complete strangers. Or rather she tried to. She'd run toward them, tail wagging madly, only to back off out of range as they reached to pet her. Then she'd prance about in a half circle, wanting to go closer, wanting to be touched, and yet afraid. Large men with facial hair were the notable exceptions. She was immediately fearful of them and kept her distance. I have no idea why. Possibly she simply never had seen any beards while in the shelter.

As she saw the same strangers for the second or third time, her trust level grew, as it did in our relationship. Naturally, her first targets became my neighbors across the road. As she streaked toward them, I'd yell, "Incoming!" and they knew what to expect. Pippa, you see, gave no warning of her approach. Never barking, she was sleek, silent, and fast. And if you saw her racing at you and didn't know her intentions, she could present a frightening sight.

Even if you recognized that she didn't present a threat, her galloping approach could be intimidating, for you didn't know what to expect upon her abrupt arrival. Would she rear up? Would she knock you down? Would she smother you with doggy kisses from a tongue that frequented places you'd rather not think about?

No. Not Pippa. Not only did she possess blinding speed; she had impressive brakes. Upon arrival just inches from my neighbors or anyone else she trusted, she'd stop abruptly, sit down, and wait to be petted. This truly was remarkable behavior to watch. And it wasn't anything that I taught her. She just seemed to come by it naturally. In fact, she never jumped up on anyone.

But people could understandably be frightened if they didn't know what she was capable of or what she intended when they saw her racing toward them. Additionally, some people just don't like dogs. That's why obedience and judicious use of the leash were important.

As I became more assured of her behavior, I allowed her off the leash more often on our walks, when other people weren't around or we travelled gravel roads with little traffic. In short order, one of her favorite activities became chasing squirrels, along with running laps and playing hide-and-seek. As a novice, she often was perplexed by the squirrels' sudden disappearance as they neared oak trees. She'd stand at the base of a tree and look around, but never up, until I called her back to resume our walk. Had she been capable, I think she would've scratched her head in befuddlement as she returned. And more than once, I imagined her suddenly asking, "Where the hell did that squirrel go?"

Over the years, dog owner friends who knew I allowed both Ursa and Pippa to run free at times on our walks told me they just couldn't risk allowing their pets off a leash or outside a fence because "they'd run off." I don't doubt that would be true for many dogs. Sometimes, the reason simply is that owners don't want to devote the time required to train their dogs to obey, whether it's to come back when called or to stop barking.

Some breeds, however, are more likely to roam. *Pet Care Facts* website lists the Lab, Jack Russell terrier, German shepherd, border collie, and husky breeds, including malamute and Akita, as some of the most common. Personally, I haven't seen that behavior in Labs, either with my own dogs or those of friends. On the other hand, I'd include the beagle as one of the most likely to take an unapproved road trip, since a typical beagle is always eager to follow its nose.

Meanwhile, chaining a dog or fencing it in a yard is intended to keep it from running away, but such practices actually increase the odds that it will, given the chance.

"They feel confined, trapped, and it drives them crazy," said the *Dog Breed Info Center* website. "They are harder to train and some appear to be literally untrainable, when really they are just going stir crazy. Most chained dogs will take off on you any chance they can get away."

Phoenix Animal Care Coalition 911 added, "The act of chaining is a huge contributor to anti-social, aggressive dog behavior. Chained dogs are 2.8 times more likely to bite than an unchained dog, not to mention the health and safety issues chaining causes the dog itself."

On the other hand, off the leash and free to run, Pippa quickly proved herself to be one sleek, silent bundle of love, racing for affection.

6. Wild Thing

"There are some dogs which, when you meet them, remind you that, despite thousands of years of manmade evolution, every dog is still only two meals away from being a wolf. These dogs advance deliberately, purposefully, the wilderness made flesh, their teeth yellow, their breath astink, while in the distance their owners witter, 'He's an old soppy really, just poke him if he's a nuisance,' and in the green of their eyes the red campfires of the Pleistocene gleam and flicker."

—Neil Gaiman and Terry Pratchett

When on a leash, Pippa walks like any other well behaved domesticated dog. Head pivoting from side to side, she keeps pace with me, occasionally falling back, drawn by a particularly appealing fragrance or to mark territory.

Off the leash, she gallops, trots, and prances, often throwing in a particularly energetic bounce for good measure, especially if she's passing a fenced yard, where another dog watches enviously. As a responsible owner and leader of our pack, I focus my attention on what she's about to do or where she's about to go and rein her in when necessary.

That's a constant challenge for she makes the Energizer Bunny look lethargic. Once she veered off into the woods toward a possum before I could even think of yelling, "Pippa! No!"

A possum has some nasty fangs, both top and bottom, and I feared the worst as they went nose to nose, an encounter filed forever in my mind's photo album of amazing moments. But all they did was sniff, look at each other curiously, and then go their separate ways, the possum resuming his search for breakfast in forest debris and Pippa bounding back to the gravel road to accompany me.

But back to my point, which is that while Pippa is off the leash, I typically don't have the luxury of observing the mechanics of her movements, as I do when we are connected. But one afternoon I did, and that's when I suddenly realized I might be sharing my home with a wolf, or, more accurately, a wolf/dog hybrid.

Pippa led the way as we walked along a path often used by deer down by the lake. She utilized none of her off-the-leash gaits. Rather she seemed deliberate and purposeful, her head straight ahead and slightly turned down. Her tail was down too, not up as it usually is when she is free and frolicking. As I walked along behind her, I noted I had seen this pace and posture before. Not from her, but elsewhere. I stopped to watch, and, suddenly, it hit me! Both in video and in real life, I had seen wolves walking exactly this way as the pack, the family, moved from one place to another, just as Pippa and I were doing now, on our way to visit a neighbor.

A wolf? Could Pippa be part wolf? And, if so, why hadn't I noticed before? Instantly, I knew the answer. Camouflage. Her black coat deflected attention from behavior that I might have noted sooner if her hair were the gray/brown and white more common to wolves. Yes, a few wolves are black, but they don't have semi-floppy ears and aren't presented as "Lab mix" at animal shelters.

But wolves are slender and have long, gangly legs, exactly like Pippa, who easily can put her front paws on my shoulders. At a little more than 45 pounds, she's on the light side for a wolf, but that could be because of whatever other genes she has.

Wolves use those long, powerful legs for speed and endurance, necessities in taking down elk, deer, or other prey. Watching Pippa pace purposefully in front of me, I realized I had seen her exhibit both traits just a few days before.

As we walked toward the end of the dam on a small lake, two does crossed from thick woods on the left to a path on the right. As with her sighting of the possum, she was lightning fast in response. In seconds, she was a silent black blur just a nose length behind two white flags.

Even more amazing, a third doe came out behind the other two and ran shoulder-to-shoulder with Pippa, without either noticing the other. Eventually, it veered off up the hill and away from her.

"If Pippa had friends that fast to help her," I remember thinking to myself, "they could catch those deer."

Fortunately, she had proven fast in another way too. Within a week or so of her adoption, Pippa responded immediately when I called her back to me during our morning and evening adventures, the sole exception being when fireworks sent her into blind panic.

When I called her off the deer, she came directly to me. And as she became accustomed to the creatures with whom we share our home territory, she decided she would rather chase and tree squirrels than pursue deer. Wild turkeys were the wild card. During our first spring together, she unintentionally flushed a hen and her young, with noisy chaos ensuing for all concerned. After retreating to the gravel road, Pippa looked up and, with her brown eyes, said, "What the hell was that?"

Along with exhibiting the speed, endurance, and posture of a wolf, Pippa also doesn't bark, even though she is capable of doing so. That's another characteristic of wolves. No, she didn't bark in the kennel, which is one of the reasons I noticed her among the canine bedlam. But twice on our walks, she voiced one short, sharp "Danger!" bark when something startled her.

Admittedly, some breeds also are less likely to bark, including pug, greyhound, Great Dane, Rhodesian ridgeback, and, of course, the basenji. The website *Adventureland Basenjis* says this: "Yes, as a general rule the basenji is the 'barkless' dog. Keep in mind that barking really has no function and is a part of the noises young dogs and pups make while developing. It is believed that most domestic dogs are trapped in adolescence because of human meddling in genetics which perpetuates the barking. The basenji originates from wild canids that do not bark. After all, silence and stealth are a key part of survival in the wild."

Also, some individuals within breeds bark less than their brethren. On the other end of the spectrum, several terrier breeds, German shepherds, basset hounds, Chihuahuas, beagles, and Pomeranians tend to bark the most.

Wolves, meanwhile, vocalize by barking, whimpering, growling, and howling. But most of the barking occurs when they're puppies. In fact, one noted expert, Dr. Temple Grandin, a professor of animal science, believes dogs are more than simply descendants of wolves; they are immature wolves, agreeing with the appraisal on the basenji website.

"Humans have neotenized dogs. Without realizing it, humans have bred dogs to stay immature for their entire lives," she said. "In the wild, baby wolves have floppy ears and blunt noses, and the grownups have upright ears and long noses. Adult dogs look more like wolf puppies than like wolf adults and act more like wolf puppies than wolf adults too. That's because dogs *are* wolf puppies. Genetically, dogs are juvenile wolves."

And, oh, yes, Pippa has a long nose, one she uses with ferocity, especially if she wants to be petted. When her snout hits your elbow, it can knock a glass out of your hand if you aren't prepared for the blow.

Additionally, as wolves evolved into domesticated animals, some animal behavior experts theorize, dogs began to bark because we designed them to do so. Those barks shared information about emotions or surroundings we understood. In other words, by the acoustic nature of the bark, we could tell if it was signifying the approach of a stranger and possible danger or a friend. It also could reveal sadness, playfulness, and happiness. From personal experience, I can tell you that Pippa's best buddy, Daisy, conveyed all of those with her barks.

On the negative side, my own belief is that some species have been inbred to the point that barking is an uncontrollable, almost neurotic behavior, and, essentially worthless in terms of communicating anything meaningful to their owners. For exhibit A, I give you Chihuahuas and most toy breeds. And for exhibit B, I give you border collies. Often on our morning walks, Pippa and I passed a border collie in a fenced yard. At least a quarter mile before we got there, the dog began barking when it heard us on the gravel road, and it continued to do so non-stop until we were a quarter mile past. It seemed as if someone had used a key to wind up the animal and it was incapable of stopping until the mechanism wound down. In addition, each bark was exactly the same and accompanied by the dog jerking up slightly, again like a windup toy.

Realizing Pippa might be more than what she appeared when I adopted her, I decided to do a little research on wolf hybrids. To my surprise, I discovered the wolador, reputedly a cross between a wolf and a black Lab. Some cynics don't think that the wolf parent of such a cross is likely to be pure, but still . . . the idea of someone intentionally creating such a hybrid stunned me.

I love wolves. I've studied them, read about them, and written novels about them. Perhaps, subconsciously, I wanted to see the wolf connection in Pippa. But I also acknowledge they are wild animals, albeit remarkable wild animals. And I don't think they should be bred with dogs to create designer pets for people. It's not the animal doing something stupid that I'm worried about. It's the people, who too often don't understand canine body language and invite trouble through careless behavior during their interactions with dogs generally—and especially with wolf/dog hybrids. For example, a hybrid almost certainly would *not* bite someone "for no reason." It would be responding to what it perceived as a threat, whether intended or not.

Still, Pippa did look exactly like a photo I found online of a wolador. And the way the owner described its behavior corresponded directly to what I'd seen in Pippa:

"She is very sweet and affectionate to her family, wary of strangers at first, but then warms up to them easily (especially when they have a dog treat). She chases almost everything." The owner mentioned her wolador features a "burnt red/brown" sheen in its black coat, a characteristic I found mentioned by several sources. Pippa has that as well. It's almost imperceptible unless you know to look for it or she is in direct sunlight.

Of course, Pippa might have no wolf in her at all. Maybe she's part greyhound, which would help explain both her build and her speed. Greyhounds typically don't bark much, and, they often require exercise to "loosen things up" before they can relieve themselves. That's certainly the case for Pippa. But generally, they have larger bone structure and weigh quite a bit more, with females typically weighing 57 to 75 pounds. Also, the greyhound is a sensitive breed that prefers peace and quiet and soft-spoken people, which perfectly describes Pippa. Then again, much the same can be said about wolves and wolf hybrids. Pippa also might be part collie, whippet, or a dozen other breeds. Who knows? Except for her sweet disposition and the color of her coat, I see little of a Lab in her, despite the shelter description of "Lab mix."

I've since learned that Lab and pit bull mixes are among the most common generic descriptions for dogs housed by shelters, especially pit bull mixes. In fairness to the shelters, they don't have enough information about the animals' ancestry to more accurately describe them. Often the dogs are strays living on the streets or abandoned by irresponsible owners.

Since adopting Pippa, I've been told by several people that I should spend $60 or more to do one of those cheek-swabbing DNA tests on her to determine what kind of "Lab mix" she truly is. And I have been tempted.

Most companies that offer this proclaim the findings are for "informational purposes only," and most owners who pay for it just want to satisfy their curiosity, with the hope that it will validate their assumptions. Still, the tests can be of real benefit for owners in determining the predominant breed of their pets. Some, such as boxers, are more prone to getting cancer and others, including Dobermans, sometimes develop bleeding disorders similar to hemophiliacs. Knowledge of these predispositions and preventative care can help keep beloved pets healthier longer.

All that being said, I'm not going to check Pippa's DNA. I don't watch interviews with actors who talk about their roles in upcoming movies. Instead, I watch the movie and enjoy it simply for what it is, not for what those who made it thought about the script and their motivations. I don't want to know what someone bought me for Christmas. I want to be surprised.

And I like not knowing if Pippa is part wolf, greyhound, Lab, or even, Heaven forbid, Chihuahua or border collie.

7. Pippa's Rules

"A dog can't think that much about what he's doing. He just does what feels right."
—*Barbara Kingsolver*

*H*aving spent her first two years of life in a shelter, Pippa was not a normal dog in a normal world when we first began exploring the woods around my house. Her life had been confined to outdoor and indoor kennels, adjacent to other dogs, with little or no exposure to the sights, sounds, and smells of nature.

And, oh, those smells. Of course, a dog's sense of smell is legendary, and for good reason. It's somewhere on the magnitude of 10,000 to 100,000 as acute as ours, according to scientists.

My friend Bob, a long-time dog owner himself, doesn't believe that statistic. "Maybe 100 times," he countered. "But it couldn't be that much."

Seeing Pippa in action twice a day, every day, I do believe the scientists.

"Let's suppose they're just 10,000 times better," said James Walker, former director of the Sensory Research Institute in an interview for NOVA on the Public Broadcasting System. "If you make the analogy to vision, what you and I can see at a third of a mile, so a dog could see more than 3,000 miles away and still see as well."

That's why dogs are used to track criminals, find lost children, detect cancer, disclose smuggled drugs, and, more recently, expose problematic zebra and quagga mussels that might be hitchhiking from one water body to another in or on boats and towed vehicles.

Even more impressive is their service to our soldiers in combat. For more than a decade dogs have saved countless lives by sniffing out improvised explosive devices (IEDs) in Iraq and Afghanistan. The military spent billions of dollars trying to develop high-tech gadgets that would do a better job, before finally deciding the best weapon against IEDs is a handler and his dog.

Which brings me back to Pippa and her discovery of our odiferous world. To anthropomorphize a bit, I'm guessing her delight must have been on a par with a child gazing upon a treasure trove of presents under the tree as he descends the steps on Christmas morning; or me stumbling upon a Snickers bar when I open the refrigerator, resigned to eating an apple for an afternoon snack.

Dogs also have extraordinary hearing, but their noses lead them, as I quickly learned while watching my adopted companion encounter the world outside concrete, gravel, and other canines. In short order, I noted her rules regarding anything she stops to smell. Pippa either rolls in it, pees on it, or eats it. I don't remember Ursa, Pippa's predecessor, or any other dog I've owned being so resolute and predictable in this behavior. Perhaps my sleek, black companion is making up for time lost—and scents missed—at the no-kill shelter.

If she decides to roll in what she sniffs, Pippa acts so quickly that it's all but impossible to stop her. In the blink of an eye, she dips and plunges her head and shoulder into the irresistible fragrance. I imagine her saying to herself: "Oh, yes, yes! This is the best! How lucky am I?"

Fortunately, because a dog's sense of smell is so much more sensitive than ours, sometimes I can't detect the slightest whiff on her hair of whatever sent her into spasms of ecstasy. Other times I'm not so lucky.

One of the most stomach-churning examples of that occurred on a day when the temperature was 15 degrees and snow blanketed the ground. Yet somehow, some way, Pippa found something wonderful (to her) in the woods behind our house, while I stacked fire wood following our walk. Unfortunately, I didn't see her do it, and so I was unprepared for what was to come.

When she came running up to me, invigorated by the cold, and eager to play, I noticed what appeared to be light brown ice on her shoulder. Without giving a thought to what it might be, I attempted to brush it off. When it didn't budge, I grasped it and pulled.

Oh, mother of God! Loosening the "ice" also set free the fragrance. And now it wasn't just on Pippa. It transferred to my glove. The closest thing I can equate it to is road kill baked in the summer sun for several days before being marinated in raw sewage. Fortunately, I don't eat breakfast until after our morning walks. Otherwise, I might have lost it. I certainly did lose my appetite. Pippa wasn't so fortunate either. When we went inside, she got a bath in doggy oatmeal shampoo, which miraculously removed the odor from her coat.

My gloves did not survive well. Following several scrubbings in hot water and soap, they still stink.

By the way, snow seems to kick up a notch Pippa's obsession with smells. Perhaps it masks older fragrances and, as a result, intensifies the fresher ones. But whether she's running, walking, or frolicking as she often does, her nose is ever alert and, most of the time, just inches from the ground. Yes, she is disciplined enough to stay reasonably close to me, but I suspect that's because she knows our routes and doesn't have to divert her attention from what's really important—the scents.

Or perhaps it's all my imagination and the actions of a black dog against a white background are more eye-catching than normal. Maybe no matter the weather conditions, she is led by her nose 99.9 percent of the time when we're outside.

What is the stinky stuff she and other dogs so delight in rolling in, whether it's on snow, grass, or leaves? I haven't a clue. Feces? A tiny dead animal? Rotten leaves? All I can tell you is that even when I can detect the odor on Pippa, I can't smell it, or see anything suspicious on the ground. Based on that, the obvious question then is: If I can smell it on her coat, why can't I find it on the ground?

What's that you say? Why am I even trying? You're right. That's the more appropriate question. Well . . . it keeps me limber.

And speaking of questions, here's another: Why do dogs roll in stinky stuff anyway? Some suspect the behavior relates to the dog's wild ancestors, who rolled in smelly debris to mask their scent for the hunt. In keeping with that theory, researchers have observed wolves rolling in animal carcasses or the droppings of plant-eating animals.

Others believe dogs like to roll in rotten and smelly stuff to "mark themselves with their most prized possessions in an attempt to show them off to their two-legged and four-legged friends." According to veterinarian Marty Becker on the *VetStreet* website,

"For a dog, wearing stinky stuff is like wearing the best designer-label scent."

Ah, yes, eau de toilette. Literally.

Becker says it's pointless trying to stop such behavior. "For you, it's foul. For dogs, it's divine," he says. "With thousands of years of practice backing their interest, dogs will continue to go boldly where no man, or woman, would ever choose to go. The only surefire way to stop the stinky sniff-and-roll is to keep your dog on the leash or teach a foolproof 'come-hither' when called."

Yeah, that latter "surefire way" might work on more portly dogs, but Pippa is lean, agile, and faster than a speeding bullet when it comes sniff, dip, and stink. Thus, I keep a bountiful supply of doggy oatmeal shampoo.

Yes, I could keep her on a leash. But I choose not to, just as I decided I won't teach her to fetch, roll over, jump through hoops, navigate an obstacle course, or any of a number of "tricks" I know she's capable of learning by virtue of her physical ability, intelligence, and disposition. Although I am firm and consistent with discipline because I want to keep her safe, you might say I'm like a parent who can't say no to his spoiled offspring. I am that way because I know how she lived for two years and I see how happy she is now, each and every day—except during thunderstorms and the Fourth of July.

I see the unbounded joy she derives from rolling on her back in green grass or brown leaves. I watch her chase a ball with wild abandon, catch it, and then throw it in the air, only to pursue it again, and finally leave it for me to pick up because she's running laps. And I feel as happy in my heart as her eyes and actions reveal her to be.

If she decides not to stop, drop, and roll on a beckoning scent, Pippa's next option is to pee on it. Not surprisingly, that is my preferred response and holds no negative consequences for me, either real—bathing a stinky dog—or imagined. I will explain the latter in a moment.

But, first, what is Pippa thinking when she pees on something? "This is my territory, dag nab it!" about sums it up.

Likely, she's squirting on top of a urine scent deposited by a dog that passed by earlier. And, just as likely, that dog was responding to the pee Pippa put there, in response to the . . . Well, you get the idea.

Whether indoors or out, dogs are territorial. Fortunately, Pippa doesn't feel the need to assert ownership inside. But outside, on the routes we regularly walk, she is relentless. I think that's why she refuses to urinate any time other than when we're walking. I've often taken her out at night, hoping to that she'll relieve herself. I've even tried leading by example. She just sits by me and watches, saving up for the next morning.

Some dog owners, meanwhile, mistakenly attribute human behavior to their pets when they do "mark" indoors. The dogs are not doing this out of jealousy or anger, but simply to assert what's theirs, especially if something new with an unfamiliar scent is introduced, such as a piece of furniture or even a pair of shoes.

According to the Humane Society of the United States, these are some reasons that dogs, both males and females, mark with urine indoors:

- Dog isn't spayed or neutered. Unneutered dogs are more assertive and prone to marking than neutered ones.
- A new pet is in the household.
- Another pet in the home is not spayed or neutered. Even spayed or neutered animals may mark in response to intact animals in the home.

- Dog has conflicts with other animals in home. When there's instability in the pack dynamics, a dog may feel a need to establish his place by marking his territory.
- Someone new is in the house (spouse, baby, roommate); dog puts his scent on that person's belongings as a way of proclaiming the house is his.
- New objects in the environment (a shopping bag, a visitor's purse) have unfamiliar smells or another animal's scent.
- Dog has contact with other animals outside home. If pet sees another animal through a door or window, he may feel a need to mark his territory.

That last one is a bit disturbing to me. Seems to me a dog who pees in the house based on what he sees out the window is in dire need of psychoanalysis—or a blindfold.

But enough about pee and stinky stuff. Let's move along to Pippa's third, and by far the most disgusting option, when she stops to smell something.

If something isn't irresistibly fragrant or in need of masking, then it must be consumed. Why? Why can't she just move on in search of the next odiferous object without gobbling it up? I wish I knew. But she won't tell me.She won't tell me, no matter how many times I yell, "No! Pippa, no! Eeeew! Pippa, why did you do that?"

Meanwhile, as I'm frightening nearby squirrels, rabbits, deer, and other woodland creatures, she grabs, gobbles, and gulps, even as she goes bounding happily ahead in search of another scent.

So, what's on the menu? Well, I've managed to intervene with Pippa enough times to spy evidence that confirms it is often excrement from woodland creatures.

Can you say "coprophasia?" That's the medical term for eating feces.

So, why does she do it? Indeed, why are 16 percent of dogs classified as "serious" stool eaters, according to a study by the

University of California/Davis? And why are 24 percent inclined to dine at least once in awhile?

"Our conclusion is that eating of fresh stools is a reflection of an innate predisposition of ancestral canids living in nature that protects pack members from intestinal parasites present in feces that could occasionally be dropped in the den/rest area," said Dr. Benjamin Hart, leader of that study.

Some, including veterinary nutritionists, suggest dogs eat the wastes of other animals to replenish enzymes so they can better digest their food. Others suspect they do so because they aren't getting enough of certain nutrients.

Then there's my own what-the-heck theory. While dogs are led by their noses, they have fewer taste buds than people. They frequently gobble down food—or feces—before they have time to chew or even taste it. So, this is what I imagine Pippa thinking when she's decided a sniff stop wasn't worth a roll or a squirt: "Well, I'm here. It's there. I might as well eat it."

Her predecessor, Ursa, was much more refined. She preferred to partake of feces only from cat litter boxes. She also ate underwear and socks left on the floor and used tissues thrown in the waste basket. And I don't even want to contemplate what she was thinking when she did so.

Whatever the reason dogs eat the disgusting things they do, the bottom line is this: They aren't going to tell us, no matter how often we ask them to explain—if you'll excuse the pun--- their shitty behavior.

And they are going to keep licking our hands and faces to show how much they love us. Remember the "imagined" consequence I was talking about? Imagine what Princess might have been eating out in the backyard just a few minutes before she gave you all those doggy kisses.

8. It's a Loud, Scary World

By Pippa

Perhaps I was brought into the shelter as a pup. Perhaps I was born there. I don't know. But I do know I spent the first two human years of my life there. That's why I survived as well as I did, I think. That's why I didn't just shut down, lie down, and die. That's why I didn't lash out in anger, growling at and trying to bite people who walked by to look at me.

I didn't know about life on the outside, except for what the other dogs told me. I didn't know about running and playing and swimming. I didn't know about toys and treats and comfy beds. I didn't know about rolling in green grass and dead leaves and fluffy snow, or even what they are. I didn't know about a world filled with smells to sniff and squirrels to chase. Other dogs who were brought into the shelter did. Some became angry. Others grew sad and depressed. They acted out. They wanted out. They missed their families, their companions, their packs. They barked and howled and snarled. Sometimes they gave up. I could see it in their eyes. It made me sad for them.

Far too many had been abandoned, dropped on the streets and forced to fend for themselves. For others, lifelong companions died and they had no place else to go. Occasionally they were brought in by humans who didn't want them anymore because they had bought new furniture or were moving and didn't want to take the dog.

Humans at the shelter cared for them, as they did for me. But most always those dogs stayed only a few months. Humans came in to look at us—them mostly. I seemed to be invisible. Then later, the dog they chose would be taken out. In fact, I saw hundreds of other dogs come and go, while I stayed. I had no idea why, and I didn't think too much about it. After all, I didn't know where those other dogs were going. Maybe it was to a worse place.

The shelter was my life. It wasn't good. It wasn't bad. It just was. It was all I knew. And, I thought, all I would ever know.

Then this human came in who actually noticed me hanging out in the back of my pen, unlike so many others who passed by, more interested in my noisy kennel mates. Because he stopped I decided to come forward. He seemed kind, much like the humans who fed and cared for me.

I was put on a leash and he took me outside. I didn't know why. We walked a little and he petted me. He wasn't mean to me, but I was afraid. He was a stranger. He petted me some more. And I wasn't as afraid. I leaned against his leg. It felt good, but still uncomfortable. I wasn't used to doing that. I don't know why I did it. Then he took me back inside and left.

But he came back! This time he took me with him. I was scared again. Where was he taking me? Were we going to where all the other dogs were taken? What happened to them? What would happen when we got there? The shelter was my home. I felt safe there. I didn't want to leave.

He took me to a place that was much larger and more open, with no other dogs there. He showed me food and water and a bed, one much softer than I was used to. Was this my home now? I didn't know if I liked it or not. He touched me and spoke in a quiet voice to me and I didn't know if I liked that either. Being so close to him still made me nervous. I might have run off and tried to find the shelter, my real home, if he allowed it. But he kept me on a leash when we went outside.

I didn't eat or drink for two days. It was all just too much for me. But going for walks—long walks—was something I quickly learned to like. I had never thought about liking anything before. My life had been about eating, sleeping, and pooping. Now I was seeing and smelling a world I had never seen or smelled. Brown, brittle things floated down from the sky. I wanted to chase them, but the leash held me back. I sniffed at them and heard them crunch when we walked on them. I liked that. Finally, I got hungry and thirsty. I ate and drank and slept on my new soft bed in my new home.

White stuff fell and felt cold on my nose. It covered the ground. I wanted to roll in it. I don't know why. Squirrels crossed the road in front of us. I knew that's what they were because of what the other dogs told me. I wanted to go after them. But my human companion kept me on the leash.

Then the day came when he allowed me off it. He set me free in front of the place I now recognized as my new home. By then, I had realized all those other dogs must have gone to new homes as well. I hoped theirs was as good as mine seemed to be.

No leash. No fences to contain me. The feeling was overwhelming. I was free! I felt frightened when taken from the shelter. Now I knew happiness. No, it was more than happiness. It was a sudden awareness. I was built to run. I was born to run. So I did. I ran and ran and ran until I could run no more. Then

I collapsed in the brown grass of my new territory and happily sucked in the cold winter air to regain my breath. I rolled on my back in the grass. Then I got up and ran some more.

But as wonderful as the outside world proved to be most of the time, sometimes it scared me. Sudden movements made me nervous. Water falling from the sky frightened me, as did an unseen force that whined as it pushed in my face, ruffled my hair, and rattled trees. Loud noises were the worst because they came without warning. I could feel them in my bones and sometimes as pain in my ears. They seemed so close and scary—I instantly wanted to run away. Inside the house, I'd hide in my crate, under the basement steps, or in the bathroom. But doing that didn't help. The noises followed me into those places.

The noises sometimes happened outside as we walked. My human companion often kept me on a leash because of this.

One early morning, I was free when I heard a sudden "Pop!" Without thinking, I ran. My companion called for me to return and I tried to obey. But then came a second noise, even more scary than the first. I ran again and this time I didn't stop. If he called after me, I didn't hear him. If there were more of those sounds, I didn't hear them either.

I ran and ran until I didn't hear the noises anymore.

PART TWO: Party Animals

9. Sherwood
By Rich Kern

The author has more than 50 years of teaching experience in public and charter schools. He is an adjunct professor at Saint Louis University in Missouri and a mathematics consultant to schools in four states. He has had a dog by his side for as long as he can remember.

I can find only one fault with dogs: They die too soon. Although, when the time is right, I believe any void left from the passing of a pet is soon miraculously filled by the unexpected arrival of a new partner. It's not necessary to search. It happens naturally because it's meant to happen. I'd like to tell you about my experience after the death of my black Labrador, aptly named by my kids, Shadow.

I volunteer each year at the public school's Camp Week, when elementary students have the opportunity to spend a week at the state park in cabins and get a taste of the outdoors. We have a ropes course, archery range, trails to hike, caves to explore, and a lake for fishing. I'm always surprised by the number of kids who've never tried any of these activities. Many have not even spent a night away from their homes. We live in a middle-class area, yet children no longer have experiences like those we had. In my day, we played until dark and explored areas miles from home on our bikes. These are different times.

On this particular Monday morning of camp, we packed the buses with eager students in high spirits, their gear, and enough food to feed the mob. Although everyone was given a packing list, a few students brought only a garbage bag with a change of clothes and a blanket. Others had enough stuff for an African safari. We tried to note those with deficiencies so we could help them out later, especially if it rained—and it always did.

We drove for a couple of hours to reach the state park. As we were assigning cabins, I saw a dog watching the process from the edge of the woods. He wasn't afraid or pushy. He just sat alertly with his ears up and his eyes following all the action. A few kids also noticed and called to him. His tail wagged and he gave us a dog smile, but continued to stay at a distance. He was a good-looking dog, most likely a Labrador mix with brown, expressive eyes and a reddish tint to his thick fur coat. I had a friend who owned a "red Lab" and he looked similar. At about 50 pounds, the dog seemed a bit thin, but his demeanor was friendly. Thinking no more about it, I told the students to get moving.

He followed us through the woods to the cabins and, again sat nearby as we arranged sleeping bags, unpacked clothes, reviewed the rules, and got ready for lunch. While my crew finished up, I stepped to the door and saw our buddy had moved a bit closer. I spoke quietly and slowly approached him. He wagged his tail and allowed me to pet him. Now openly friendly, he leaned into my touch. That's when I noticed the poor fellow was covered with ticks, his eyes were matted, and he was a bit thin. He was a lot of love in a well-worn package. I picked off 10 or 20 of the blood-suckers, but barely made a dent.

He was a sad sight, but as the kids surrounded him, his grin returned and he was in heaven with all the attention. Without really intending to, we seemed to have adopted him. Or he adopted us. At lunch, he waited outside and then followed my group of nine as we exited the chow hall and hiked toward a local cave. The trip was maybe a mile and a half. I think he recognized our destination because he soon took the lead and ran ahead. Then he stopped to wait for us, before charging ahead again. He did this several times, always making sure we were close behind.

That night at the bonfire, Tracy, another volunteer, and I picked ticks off him for more than an hour. Finally, we were starting to get most of the bigger ones, but I knew he was covered deep in his fur. I could tell he'd been on his own in the woods for some time. We did this every night until he tired of us and walked a few yards away to flop down. During the day when the kids began to get on his nerves, he crawled under a truck or bus just out of reach, but never too far, so he still could see all the action.

Not surprisingly, our new companion also hung around during meal times. Camp food may be edible, but it bears a disturbing resemblance to school cafeteria lunches. That's why experienced volunteers bring supplementary fare, which they gobble while the kids eat their supper. One night, I was putting a couple of burgers on my hibachi when I suddenly had the uncomfortable feeling someone was staring at me. I looked up to see sad, brown eyes looking at me expectantly. I threw on a third burger. He became my constant dinner companion after that. We shared peanut butter crackers, Fritos, and the main course each night.

During the next three days, we never separated. He slept on the porch of our cabin, followed us to every destination, and the

students dubbed him Sherwood, a noble, distinctive name that somehow reflected his personality. The park ranger told us Sherwood had been dropped off about eight weeks earlier and they were hoping someone would take him home. Prodded by adults and students, I was easily persuaded.

On Friday, our last morning, there was no Sherwood and everyone started to worry. Kids had tears in their eyes, and a search proved to be futile. Teachers, volunteers, and about 150 kids spread out to cover all the trails, every building, and the lake where we went fishing. No Sherwood. I'm sure his new name was called thousands of times, but he was nowhere to be found. Finally, we ran out of time and called an end to the search. Of course, it also was raining. We packed the bus with muddy clothes and muddy kids and even muddier spirits. It was time to leave.

That night was tough for me. I certainly didn't go to camp looking for a new dog, but this one just seemed to be right. The next morning, I decided to go back to the park. The campground felt empty and weird without all the kids. I hiked the same areas we'd searched the day before, calling for Sherwood. Two hours later, I was hoarse and figured it just wasn't meant to be. Not a single sighting or distant bark. I just hoped he wasn't somewhere hurt. I got back in my truck to go home.

I was dejected as I drove back to the park entrance, but that's when fate took over. About 100 yards from the park entrance, Sherwood broke from the woods right in front of my truck, as though he knew this was his last chance. I stopped the truck, jumped out, and we hugged each other, both of us happy as we could be. Sherwood found me!

He sat in the passenger seat as we drove to my vet, who scanned for a chip just in case, but he didn't have one. He did need some medical care and we spent time combing even more ticks out of his coat, getting his vaccinations and other shots for infections, all before giving him a much-needed bath. He still needed future healing, but he was ready to meet his new family as I drove us home. That was eight years ago; we are now pack.

10. Brown Dog
By Steve Chaconas

The author, Captain Steve Chaconas, is a former business radio talk host in Washington, DC. He now is a bass fishing guide on the Potomac River, as well as an outdoors writer. He has been featured in TV, radio, and print and twice was the Fox News Sunday "Power Player of the Week."

When I was growing up, dogs were a small but memorable part of my life. Then for years, they weren't even a consideration. Surprisingly, after several dogless decades, my wife and I are now dog people.

My mother had a super intelligent, award-winning purebred poodle named Wonder. He was a neurotic show dog—an angry dog, not a cuddle pooch. This high-maintenance fluffy dog bit anything that moved. I entertained my eight-year-old buddies by moving a chair to witness Wonder angrily attack the legs. Our next dog was another crazy canine, picked up Turkey, where my dad was stationed in the Air Force. I'm guessing it was a cross between a collie and a pit bull. He would herd me into a corner and then attack. His Turkish name was Tamam. Before we knew the English translation, we took him home. Tamam in Turkish roughly means *finish*, as in kill or destroy. My advice: Find out the origin of a dog's name before allowing it to sleep with you. When we left Turkey, we left Tamam with another military family.

Decades and lots of cats later, my wife and I enjoyed a bark-free home. No fence required, no leashes or walking. Without children, we were free to leave for days and even a week or so with no worries. A bucket of water, a food feeder, and a few extra litter boxes and we hit the road. My wife retired two years ago and we built a home in the mountains. Life was good. As the mountain house was nearing completion, my wife and niece Amanda, who was living with us at the time, overtly conspired (or threatened) they were getting a dog. I countered with all the reasons a dog wasn't right for us. Who would feed it? Who would walk it? Who would clean up the poop? Not me, for sure.

Then one day my wife came home with a brown dog. She might have brought a black Lab, a chocolate Lab, or a yellow Lab. Instead, she brought a meth lab! The dog was wild. We couldn't train a dog like this with dog biscuits. We had to hook him up with Sudafed. He yipped and barked. He attacked any loose object including, but not limited to, shoes, pens, and glasses. I hid my Maui Jim sunglasses, but lost my favorite fishing hat.

My safe house was under siege. Accustomed to leaving fishing gear all over, now I had to puppy-proof my living space. Although it was impossible to cat-proof a house because nothing is out of their reach, we found sanctuary from the brown dog by moving our valuables to higher ground. Brown Dog couldn't jump.

Even my gardens weren't safe from this digging, chewing machine. Carefully cultivated 30-year-old azaleas were no match for the brown jaws of destruction. A beautiful wooden fence served as a backdrop to more gardens, while providing privacy. Finding the bottom of the fence to be shovel ready, Brown Dog excavated in an attempt to visit neighboring dogs. The escape from Alcatraz had nothing on this tunneling terrier.

As it began to settle in that I was now a dog person, we had to decide on a name. Brown Dog worked for a while, but the rescuers had named him Franklin. The foster home kept the name. The first adoptive family kept the name before turning him back over to animal rescue. That was our first warning. Back to another foster home and then to us, Franklin found his forever home.

Naming a cat had been easy. Animals normally make me laugh so we chose comedian names. Cats named Stan and Ollie, Jerry Lewis, Sid Caesar, Chevy Chase, and Tina Fey have shared their home with us. Now we were tasked with justifying Franklin or changing his name. I suggested, Dice, as in Andrew "Dice" Clay. Noting this comic's vulgarity, my wife declined. One of my favorite comics in the 70s, whom I met in the 90s, was Franklin Ajaye. Franklin would work. But to me and my friends, he was still Brown Dog.

Since we were relatively novice dog owners, school was in order. We found out quickly that Brown Dog loved anything with a pulse and became the canine class clown. He obeyed for a few seconds and then encouraged his buddies to break rank and eye contact on their way to mischievous antics. A diploma was awarded, if not deserved. He sits when he wants. He stays when he wants. And he heels when he wants. Trouble is he doesn't want to sit, stay or heel that often. He does eat on command.

Many dogs find their safe space in plastic crates and metal kennels. Not Brown Dog! My wife tried the crate. She slept on the couch next to the crate; otherwise Brown Dog whimpered and howled. This lasted a few weeks. Then she brought the crate into our bedroom. After a few days, Brown Dog ended up on our waterbed. At first it was interesting to see him attempt to walk. Soon after he gained his sea legs, he felt at home.

Before my wife brought home Brown Dog, the cats were a primary reason I put up an anti-mutt offensive. Cats are quiet and they hide. Dogs can't hide; they need attention and make this need known. My Fey cat is afraid of her shadow. With the introduction of Brown Dog, Fey took refuge in my office, which was off limits to the chewing dog. Our attention turned to our house kitty, Chevy. He'd never seen a dog before. Curious at first, he now has a playmate. The dog loves to chase and Chevy often turns the tables.

Finding that dogs will eat anything, we set up a special cat-only room, with food, water, and litter box. Brown Dog succeeded in avoiding the barrier to find cat food treats in the food bowl . . . and in the litter box. We constructed a bigger wall.

Like cats, dogs eat out of bowls. That's where the similarity ends. Cats nibble, so leaving food in a feeder works. Brown Dog ate all the food at once and then chewed the bowl.

Cats will only chase what they can catch and kill. Brown Dog wants to chase cars. And riding with him in one for three hours to our mountain home presented another challenge. Our first trip included projectile vomiting. Fortunately Brown Dog and I now are on the same bathroom break schedule. After we fasten his seatbelt and he creates a bed, Brown Dog makes the trip quite well, sleeping most of the way. Nowadays, he is a patient passenger until he hears the turn signal, indicating frequent turns as we approach home.

We aren't sure which he likes best, our suburban or country home. Suburbia requires a leash, walking on sidewalks, looking out for other dogs, kids, and cars, and picking up poop. In the country, long leash or loose leash walks are in order, while leaving the poop behind. Visits from our friends George and Betty and Molly, their border collie/Mountain Feist mix, allow both dogs to run through our orchard and around the pond. Brown Dog now is a social member of the family.

He quickly learned his name, as a treat was readily dispensed by his "mom." He learned to fetch, again a treat. He liked to play tug of war; more treats. Sit up and beg? Not quite. This spoiled little Brown Dog turns down Milk Bones just to get his way. We've tried reasoning with him, by giving him the "dogs are starving in Africa line." He looks at us and can tell we don't miss any meals, so he knows there's no starving to worry about at our house.

Meanwhile, I've learned a new language. I now speak doggy. No matter the breed, where they were raised or the temperament, they all respond to "Good boy" or "Good girl." This is especially useful when encountering the unleashed. A well timed "Good boy" will cause any dog to pause, tilt his head, and wonder how I knew what to say to him. Additionally, tails are a form of communication. When a cat has its tail up high, it signals contentment. If the cat's tail is twitching, it's a warning to stay away. As I've learned from Brown Dog, dogs aren't quite so skilled. If his tail is wagging, he might be just fine. Or he might be hungry. He might be agitated or need to go to the bathroom. Or he might be hungry. Still, tail wagging or not, dogs are usually happy to see you—and usually hungry.

Cats will purr and rub against your leg. Be alarmed when the purring stops. They are up to something. Dogs will rub up against you, sometimes not socially acceptable, and even bark to get your attention. This is a sign of affection, or could be they are hungry. Dogs are honest pets. They look you in the eye, letting you know they like you, trust you, or they're hungry. If a cat looks you in the eye, it's just measuring the distance to your nose from its claws.

The old saying, "The way to a dog's heart is through its stomach," never rang truer than with Brown Dog. I have resisted sharing table food with him and can now say "no" to puppy dog eyes. Not so easy, but for his own good. There are things a dog should never eat in spite of their willingness to devour anything, including the buffet in the litter box. Everyone knows about chicken bones, chocolate, and nuts. I wanted to be a good dog owner, so I did a search and found that alcohol, tobacco, and coffee are not good. Now both of us are trying to quit. These items certainly make sense, but others I had to think about. Onions and garlic, for instance. Who would feed those to a dog? Their breath is bad enough to begin with. Corn will block the intestines, and make pooper scooping more challenging.

I asked my vet why dogs roll over. He said it's either a learned behavior bred into the canine species over thousands of years of domestication with the dog showing subservience to his human master, or it might just be they like to have their bellies rubbed. In either case, I've learned to rub Brown Dog's belly, a definite no-no with a cat, where there's a guarantee of a scratch or two.

Cats constantly clean themselves. They do not require bathing, nor is any attempt to do so safe. After a few, "What's that smell?" conversations with my wife, we realized dogs need a bath every once in awhile. Cats groom, dogs lick. Don't get me wrong, dogs are fairly hygienic, but they focus their licking attention only on specific areas. Good thing, because I'm not washing him there anyway. I know this and yet I still let Brown Dog lick my face.

Walking a cat on a leash doesn't impress anyone. It's not actually walking; it's drag and stop, and then pick up and carry home. Dog walking can be exercise for both of you. Walking Brown Dog not only enables a decent cardio workout twice a day, but also provides upper body workouts as I pull him away from other dogs, people, and well-manicured gardens.

Dogs are genuine, Brown Dog included. He wants to be involved in every activity. Yard work, he chases leaves. Washing the car, he grabs the hose. Cooking, he eats what I accidentally, or intentionally, drop. Cats tease you, pretending to be interested and then they walk away, slowly.

My wife got Brown Dog primarily because all our cats eventually gravitated to me. Now, after two years, Brown Dog sleeps next to me. He chose my lap as the only one for him. And he loves to hang out when I'm working on my boat or fishing tackle. I put a dog toy on a line with a fast reel and make casts to play with him.

I even take him for walks and pick up his poop. Watching other dog owners, I learned there's a technique to this. Turn the bag inside out and then place a hand inside the bag to grab the plopper and allow the bag to roll over it. This allows a knot to be tied to seal for the trash can. I'm over the gagging part of that, and it actually feels warm in the colder months.

Now that Brown Dog and I have become friends, I've noticed we are starting to look alike. His brown hair is getting a bit lighter and thinner. His belly is extending below his harness, and, when in the car, we both squint to see what's up ahead. When we're alone, Brown Dog sits on my lap and watches *Bassmaster TV* with equal interest and probably equal comprehension. Who was rescued is up for debate. The brown dog is now a good boy.

11. Opry
By Randy Joe Heavin

The author is a singer/songwriter whose song, "I Wanna Go Fishing," has become the anthem for anglers everywhere. He retired from the U.S. Air Force as a Senior Master Sergeant. He is an avid tournament fishermen and expert martial artist.

At any given second, forces can act upon a person's life and change it beyond his comprehension. For me, that force came in the form of small, scraggly, black Lab puppy. Back in 2000, Mike, an old Air Force buddy, was visiting me for the weekend and—because he was a harmonica player—we decided to attend a local Saturday night blues jam in hopes he could sit in with the band. Because the jam didn't get cranked up until 10 p.m. and we had time to kill, we thought it would be cool to take in a country music show at the Oklahoma Opry.

After the show was over and while waiting in line to exit the building, I noticed a small puppy had found sanctuary from the wind and icy rain by crawling into the small space between a glass door and the exterior wall. As people pushed open the door to leave, they inadvertently sandwiched the cold pup against the wall, making it hard for him to retreat. As I got closer to the door, I grabbed it and held on so as to not squish the little guy.

I'll never forget the scared look in that pup's eye as I knelt down and reached behind the door to pet him. He was wet and shaking, yet he trusted me enough to allow it. I gently wiped some of the water off his face and head while at the same time speaking to him in what seemed to be some sort of childish new voice not normally coming from this man. My words were something on the lines of "easy boy, good dog," and "you poor little guy."

I held the door until all the people left and, sometime during those few minutes, the little pup walked over and sat against my kneeling leg. Mike chuckled and said, "He's a perfect fit. You should take him home."

I looked up at Mike and said, "It's not going to happen."

Time was passing and there wasn't any more reason to stay, so I suggested we get a move on so we could make the jam. I petted the pup one last time and then we headed for my truck.

After we ran through the rain and got into the truck, once again Mike started in on me about taking the dog. He said, "You live alone and need something to care for."

I told him I always wanted a German shepherd and was going to hold out for that type of dog. I felt victorious at staving off my friend's attempts at locking me down with some four-legged responsibility. Rain still poured hard as we pulled out of the lot and headed toward the blues bar. Next stop: girls and great music.

The intersection was just a few hundred yards away, and the light was green. Just as I started to accelerate I noticed movement in the street, so I slammed on the brakes. The little pup had run down the street and was now directly in my path. I couldn't believe it. Mike laughed, again insisting I take the dog home, and said, "It's fate."

"No! I don't want him," I said.

After, some back and forth, my old friend made his point by pulling on my heart strings. I yelled, "Okay. Okay. You get the damn dog and put him in the back, and I'll find him a home later."

Mike grabbed the dog and put him in the back. I had a camper shell so he stayed nice and dry. When Mike got back in the truck, I noticed he had mud on his shirt. It was at that point I knew our night of fun was over and had taken an entirely different direction than I wanted.

We headed back to the house with Mike's harmonicas and my new puppy. I had a dog. Just great!

I decided to clean the little stray right away and I told Mike he was going to help me. At home, I opened the camper shell to grab the dog and I noticed the craziest thing. I could already see some sort of renewed life in the pup's demeanor. He was looking directly into my eyes and it was as if he was saying, "I knew you would come."

We put the dog in the bathtub and he didn't seem to mind at all. We gave him a good wash down and removed about eight or nine ticks. During the wash, Mike told me we needed to name the dog. I insisted there was no point to naming him because I wasn't keeping him and the new owner may not like our choice.

Mike laughed as he said, "Yeah, right. You're keeping him."

I avoided the name thing until Mike suggested I call him Opry after the Oklahoma Opry where we found him. That suggestion actually made sense and the name was kind of cool, so I agreed. Opry became his name. I lost several arguments that night. Lucky me.

After the bath I picked Opry up from the tub and put him on the floor. Again he looked me directly in the eye and then boom!

He was off and running. He ran through the house like he was rocket propelled. He barked and yelped. I swear I could almost hear him saying, "Yahoo!"

Mike and I couldn't help but laugh as we watched Opry run like he'd just been freed from doggy prison. In a sense, I guess he was. I mean losing two or three pounds of mud and a bunch of ticks, along with getting out of the icy rain would make me happy too.

The next morning I woke to find Opry on my bed and at my feet. To be honest, there was something cool about seeing that little stray curled up, warm, and safe. Little did I know, Opry was staking his claim. I happened to glance over at the clock and then it hit me. I had slept for seven hours and surely a mess would be waiting for me. I jumped up and checked the house for puppy poo packages. There were none. Good boy!

It was Mike's last day to visit and he'd already packed up to leave. He said, "You make sure and keep that dog."

I told him the dog was gone as fast as I could find it a home. He laughed .

After a few weeks passed, Mike called and asked, "How's your dog doing?"

I said, "It's not my dog and I am getting rid of him as soon as I can find him a home."

He laughed. "Sure you are!"

That same exchange played out over and over for several months. In fact, many of my friends started asking me how I liked having a dog. I kept saying, "I'm getting rid of that damn dog!"

Funny thing is, the only home Opry ever managed to find was mine. And Mike knew that all the time.

About a month or two after I brought Opry home, I figured I should take him to the veterinarian for a checkup and shots. He estimated Opry to be a couple months old and said he was born sometime near January or February. I told the vet to log his birth date as Feb. 11, the same day as mine. Over the next few months, Opry began to grow on me and I found myself looking forward to getting home from work. I couldn't wait to see how happy he was each time I walked in. Opry claimed the corner of the sofa and that spot put his view in direct line with the door. Each time I entered the laundry room from off the garage, I heard his tail slapping the back of the sofa long before I got to the door leading to the living area. Once inside the second door, I could see him looking right at me from his spot. I just didn't know how fast this pup would get to my heart and change my life. Opry had special power in his big brown eyes.

As time passed, Opry and I grew closer. We adapted to one another perfectly. I taught him and he learned. He would climb things on request. When I asked him if he wanted to walk me, he would go get the leash and I would clip it around my neck. He would take the end in his mouth and pull me around the coffee table.

At Christmas, Opry would wait by the tree to open presents he knew were there for him. I would tell him to get a gift and he would do so. I told him to pull off the bow and open the gift, and he'd do that with all the excitement and exuberance of a kid opening gifts from Santa.

Yes, Opry was an amazingly smart creature and the best friend anyone could ask for. He found a place deep in my heart. Still, for years, I continued telling people I was getting rid of him. But they knew Opry was my dog and he wasn't going anywhere except on road trips, fishing trips, truck rides, and walks around the neighborhood.

The adventures Opry and I shared were almost too much to believe. Some might say certain events sound like part of a movie.

However, the stories are facts, laced with what I believe to be divine intervention.

Once, on a road trip to Illinois, I stopped at a gas station on the highway near St. Louis. As I was pumping gas, Opry jumped out of the truck and took off running toward the on ramp. I yelled, but he kept running. That dog loved to run. I had to hurry and pay for the gas before going after him. It only took seconds to pay, but it felt like hours. I ran to the truck and pulled  over to the ramp, yet I couldn't see Opry anywhere. I was nervous and a tad frantic. I pulled up on the highway to get a better vantage point, but nothing. I drove down the highway about a quarter mile and pulled over. I couldn't see my buddy anywhere. I was truly scared. Just as panic set in, a stranger pulled up to me, which put me on guard. But then he asked if I was looking for a dog.

I thought this couldn't be real. What made this guy think I was looking for a dog? What are the odds? It could be a trick. But I was looking for a dog, so I listened.

He said there was a black dog behind the fence at the propane plant on the service road. It sounded too good to believe, but I had a lot to lose, so I decided to check it out. I crossed over the highway and jumped on the service road going the other direction. The propane plant wasn't very far and I could see it. As I pulled up, I notice the facility had white tanks set in white gravel. I could instantly see a dark contrasting object moving about the place, and it looked like a dog. No way! As I got closer, Opry noticed it was me and started running along the fence line barking and waggling his tail as if it were all a game. I wasn't laughing, but I got my boy back. I sure dodged a big heartache here. Luck or divine intervention?

As if one close call on a road trip wasn't enough, the powers to be decided to test Opry and me again. Would you believe it was on another road trip to Illinois to visit Mom? My Uncle Joe was also visiting on this trip and he fancied himself quite the dog handler. I went over to my brother's for a few hours and felt okay leaving Opry with Mom. Before I left, I remember insisting that if anyone took Opry for a walk they should not to let him off the leash because he would run.

But Uncle Joe thought it would be okay to let Opry off the lead so he could run and play. It took him only a second to realize he made a huge mistake as Opry disappeared into the neighborhood. When my uncle couldn't find my dog, he decided he'd better call me to assist. I was furious. My main problem wasn't so much that he let Opry off the lead, but that he waited a good half hour before letting me know. Opry had a good head start.

If only a minute or two had passed, I wouldn't have worried as much. But this was a strange area and 30 minutes was a long time to run. It was getting dark and, adding to my concern, was the fact that this wasn't the neighborhood of yesteryear. The cocker spaniels and collies that once graced local backyards had been replaced by pit bulls, and lots of them.

An hour or so passed as I searched and searched with no luck. This time I thought Opry was gone forever. I called my brother, who was looking too. I told him I was going up to State Street. He cautioned me to not spend too much time in that area, because crossing State would put me in one of the most violent neighborhoods in the county.

I told him I'd be careful, but I had to look. I searched right up to State and started to return, but something inside me said, "You must continue." I drove into the urban danger zone. As I went down a hill, this clearly wasn't a place where I belonged. Still, I continued. In about a half mile, I came to a social gathering on the side of the street—a sort of block party. People looked at me and I thought, "I'd better get the hell out of there because I'm not welcome."

It really hit me then that Opry was gone. But as I turned around the truck, I heard a familiar bark. Then I saw him tied to a fencepost way out in someone's backyard. No freaking way could this be!

I drove my truck down an alley that went behind the homes. As I pulled up near the post where Opry was tied, I spotted some guys who appeared to be gang members on the porch and each held a lead attached to a pit bull.

I'm sure they were going to use my pup in a fight and I wasn't about to let that happen .My heart raced as I jumped out of the truck and grabbed Opry's lead. I made no attempt to untie it. I just quickly pulled out my knife and cut it. I picked up my dog and hurled him over my shoulder and into the truck. I followed as quickly as possible and we sped out of there at warp speed. Lucky for us, those guys never set the pit bulls free. I saved this dog for a third time! Luck or divine intervention?

I could detail story after story about the crazy experiences Opry and I shared over his lifetime. But the main point I hope to convey is that something brought us together not once, but time and time again. This relationship between man and dog was written in the cards. He was sent to save me, and I him. We became friends loyal to the core, a perfect match. I could have just walked right out that door and passed that pup like all the other people that rainy night, but something made me stop. I could have driven on down that street and not given a second thought about stopping to pick him up, but my friend pushed me. I could have ignored that strange man who stopped on the side of the road in St. Louis to ask if I was looking for a dog, but something made me listen. And something made me heed my gut and my heart, which told me to cross into the most dangerous of neighborhoods to find my dog. The pieces always seemed to fall into place with Opry and me, and life was good until . . .

In June of 2016, I woke up early to let Opry outside. As he was walking back to the house, he collapsed and couldn't get up. He was disoriented and had no balance. I ran out to help him. I cradled his tummy to get him up and help walk him into the house. I could tell something wasn't right.

I put him up on his spot on the couch with the hope he would regain his balance. For a few hours he tried, but his body just wouldn't cooperate. I petted him and talked to him for a few hours, but he never seemed to recover. For the first time in more than 16 years, I could see the tiredness in his eyes. It was killing me, but he was telling me the time had come.

I called the veterinarian and we agreed he had a stroke. Because of Opry's age and his other medical conditions, I was forced to make the decision I dreaded for several years. I had to let him go. Upon request, the vet came to my house.

This was, by far, the hardest thing I have ever done, but I knew Opry couldn't go on like that. The vet was a real pro, kind and gentle. She respected my buddy and my love for him. With tears falling, I kissed Opry on the head, and said," I will always love you, boy."

I honestly feel he knew what was going on and was ready. He looked at me one last time and I'm sure I heard him say, "I love you too," before he closed his eyes and returned home.

Six months have passed since my best friend left this world, but I still feel him close. Often, I find myself talking to him. My life just isn't the same now.

People want me to get another dog, but at this point, I just can't. Maybe when I'm in another house it will be okay, but this is Opry's place. During our 16 1/2 years, Opry and I took a lot of road trips to see my Mom in Illinois. I had him cremated and took him back there with me. I stopped off at all the places where we used to stop and walk. I carried him with me up a hill to the trees and to a lookout point he liked. Some might think it's silly to do such a thing, but I needed it. Real animal lovers will understand.

I loved that dog, and still do. It would be easy to be bitter, but I just can't be. I was lucky. No, *we* were lucky. We shared more than 16 years of laughter, loyalty, and love. I can't see sadness through all the wonderful memories. I love all the forces that brought that dog into my life. There was no better match to be made between man and dog than Opry and me. RIP ole buddy. We will play again.

12. Sampson
By Judy Tipton

The author is a dog lover, inventor and, conservationist who lives on her family farm in Christiansburg, Kentucky.

*T*he first time I saw him, he was a long-eared black and white pup who often roamed the farmer's field adjacent to his comfortable brick home. He belonged to a neighbor in our rural farming community. The Andersons are a nice family with children and one day a car stopped by loaded with puppies for adoption and their children eagerly agreed to take one. They named him Sampson.

Sampson's first love is children. So, when the sounds of playing and laughter radiated up the small hill to their home from the start of Sunday

School at Christiansburg Baptist Church, Sampson made his way down to join the fun. This soon became his weekly ritual.

Early in Sampson's life, the Andersons had to move to "town," as folks call it around here. They were moving closer to work and into a golf course community that didn't allow dogs. The Andersons wanted what was best for Sampson, and understanding his love of attending church every Sunday, decided it was best to give him to another neighbor.

I don't know the reason. It may have been that Sampson wanted to be near his former home or closer to the church, but the new neighbor arrangement didn't work for Sampson. Soon he became the neighborhood dog referred to commonly as the "church dog."

Although his original family moved, Sampson made himself a life in the small community of 10 or so houses. Doing his own thing, independent of ties of one family, Sampson quickly befriended everyone. You see, Sampson has this charisma. Maybe he learned how to be a good neighbor and get along well with others at church. I don't know. But all the people of Christiansburg loved him, and so did all the other dogs. Sampson could pass through any yard without resistance.

Fran Smith, an elderly lady, let Sampson in at night so he had a couch to sleep on. Earl Tipton, a widower living alone, always made breakfast for two, complete with eggs, bacon, and coffee. Sampson was there morning after morning at 7:30 sharp. Joe Miller made a bed under his back porch, so when a storm blew in Sampson had a dry place to ride it out. And every Sunday, Sampson went to church.

This is where I come into the story. Living back on my family farm with my mother after my father's death, we had four dogs. We always had dogs. But neighbor Joe explained to my mother that he and his wife were selling their home to move into an assisted-living apartment and he was distraught about what would happen to Sampson after he moved away.

My mother quickly eased his worries. Registered at the Shelby County Dog License office, Sampson became ours and a trip to the vet assured he was up to date on all his shots. But the transition to a new and permanent home wasn't easy at first. There were many late night drives around the neighborhood looking for Sampson, to bring him in so he'd be safe from coyotes. He did finally learn to join the walks with our other four dogs back on the farm each day. But he was still set on eating breakfast at Earl's and attending church on Sunday.

As Sampson settled more into his new home and life on the farm, and with the passing of both Fran and Earl, Sampson left his roaming days behind him, except for his Sunday ritual.

Sampson is possibly a border collie mix. If you're familiar with the breed, then you know border collies need jobs. They need to work. So, with curiosity getting the best of me, I followed Sampson to church one morning to see how his day went. Little did I know, he was an usher. Sampson would greet a family in the parking lot and walk them to the church door. Then he returned to the lot to escort another family.

After all the folks went inside, Sampson lay under one of the stained glass windows. To my surprise, when the choir started to sing, Sampson whirled around in circles and then harmonically joined in, howling. He was a choir member, too. When church was over, Sampson walked his fellow congregation members back to their automobiles, until everyone had left. Then he returned home around 12:20 p.m. Sampson did this faithfully through heat, cold, rain, or snow for 13 years.

No one knows Sampson's exact age. But if I were to guess, he's around 15 years old now. Two years ago, after the preacher retired,

Sampson decided it was time for him to retire also. He no longer makes the Sunday trip to church, but church members often stop by to inquire about him or even send him cards to say they miss him.

Sampson is having a wonderful retirement with an orthopedic bed for watching TV and daily naps and another in his upstairs bedroom. His daily meal consists of toast for breakfast and a cooked chicken breast, rice, and dog food mixture every night for dinner. He enjoys being hand fed a few biscuit treats as well. Oh, and he still makes those daily walks on the farm.

No, this is not another sad dog story. This is the story of the happy and charmed life of Sampson the Church Dog.

13. Bear

By Blake Muhlenbruck

The author lives near the foothills of northern Colorado with his wife, daughter, and two dogs, Nala and Nox. Despite a debilitating industrial accident in 2002, he is an avid outdoorsman, inventor, inspirational speaker, artist, and author.

*L*ovey and Duffus, two rat terriers, gave me my first realization of what the word "companion" means. Forty acres of Colorado mountainous terrain with rattlesnakes, bobcats, mountain lions, and bears should have been enough to keep most parents from letting their kids outdoors, let alone a seven-year-old with a severe hearing impairment. But my parents gave me full run of the land, with my BB gun in hand and my two trusted companions.

We had great adventures in the wild. I spent my time pretending I was Grizzly Adams without his unforgettable beard, an innocent fugitive on the run who befriended a grizzly bear as his companion. Ben, his bear, alerted ol' Adams of impending danger and where to find food and shelter. In each episode, Adams and Ben saved some unsuspecting soul from a horrible fate, with a valuable life lesson at the end. The three of us learned from Adams and Ben to always check for ticks.

When I was a teen, we had more of a zoo than a farm. Doobie dog, a stray of sorts, was our neighbor's Doberman Pinscher, who found her way over our fence one day and never left. One Eyed-Beth was a rescued greyhound who lost one eye chasing a rabbit during a race. For my 16th birthday I received a Shih Tzu mix named Panda, a pup from my first love and girlfriend, Crystal. Panda taught me another lesson in companionship: Girls come and go, but dogs remain loyal.

Age brought responsibilities, including a family and home filled with children and animals as the cycle of life continued. Shadow was a Keeshond who ventured into my gas plant workplace office— and into my heart. That night, I searched in vain for her owner, stopping at each farmhouse to ask about a missing dog. "Nope," was the unanimous answer. So our little family grew by one. My first wife wasn't nearly as excited about Shadow as my daughter and I were, but that was okay. We had our Shadow. Panda, Fancy (our momma cat), and Pickle (her kitten) got a new companion as well; they all became best buddies. Our daughter learned her first lesson in death after Shadow ate her hamster. And I was reminded yet again about companionship: Wives come and go, but dogs stay by your side. Sadly, the dogs do no live long enough.

Years later I married my second wife, also a dog lover, and we added to our own litter, making three daughters in total. We were set with a new life, a new home, and a new career. We decided early on that one of us would stay home and take care of our brood. She would leave her job as a hotel general manager and I'd be the bread winner, working as an oil and gas industrial expert.

As they say, "History repeats itself." Soon after moving into our new home, we decided the girls should experience a real pet. Nipples, their Beta fish, wasn't very interactive. A trip to the local mall gave us Niko, a rambunctious little fur ball who knocked out our middle daughter's front tooth. In May of 2000, just two months after joining our family, Niko passed away from parvo. No more pet store animals, we decided, after finding the pet store owner never gave the proper shots.

We waited two years before getting another pet, and because parvo can live in the soil for many years. First, we adopted three kittens from my parents' farm. Ashley and Grace were sisters, and Candy, our male, was from a different momma. Notice the name Candy? Obscure names happen when children name the family pets. Gender makes no difference.

Two years from the day of Niko's passing, we visited our local shelter instead of a pet store. At the time, our shelter was a hopeless place where only a lucky few animals were adopted. Undersized, understaffed, and underfunded, they had no choice but to put a time limit on life. At times the wind carried the stench of the cremated bodies for miles, reminding the city of its less fortunate citizens. We saw adopting a dog from there as a way of saving a life, plus an opportunity to gain a lifetime family member. We wanted a dog our girls could spend years with, having adventures together and learning the responsibilities that come with having a companion.

As we walked through back halls of a bleak, dimly lit passage to the large breed holding area, the concrete held the pungent odor of urine, feces, and bleach. The stench nearly took our breath away. In one of the holding cells was a black and white mix with long hair named Wiggles because of his out of control movements. In the other was a small, scrawny, and shaky Lab/German shepherd mix named Floppy because of his ears. A worker asked if we would like to see either pup. Our girls chose the black and white first. Led to a back room, we awaited its arrival. Bursting into the room was a crazy mutt with no manners and not a care in the world. Our daughters fell in love, begging ensued—"Please, Daddy, please!"

But we hadn't seen the other pup, so I rained on their parade. I saw something in him that told me we should consider him as well. Calm and cool instead of rambunctious, he seemed to instantly take to the girls. We discussed the situation and decided Floppy would come home with us that night. "Not so fast," the worker told us. We spent so much time with the dogs, the workers had closed the cash register for the day. We would have to wait until the next morning. Sad faces looked up at my wife and me. My wife asked if we could put a hold on him.

"No, first come, first serve with no guarantee he'll be here when you come tomorrow," the worker said. I explained I had to work the next day. I hoped our pleas wouldn't go unnoticed, but I could tell my crying kids didn't touch her heart either. "Rules are rules," she said.

Leaving empty-handed, we needed a plan to get Floppy the next day. "You will rush home from work and I'll have my grandmother watch the kids," my wife said. "We'll drive fast. We will have positive thoughts all day, and it will turn out great!" Additionally, the shelter received a call every hour on the hour that entire day from us. I'm sure they were amused.

"Twenty minutes till they close. Drive like I'm in labor!" my wife said when I arrived home from work. I did as I was told. Inside, the shelter workers were waiting for us with Floppy and a stack of paperwork. I handed over a check. Floppy was ours.

"Hey, do you know how lucky this dog is?" a worker asked. "In the morning he was going to be put to sleep. He's been here for a long time. Guess it is his lucky day." My wife and I both swallowed hard.

On our way home, we picked up burgers and fries, supposedly because there was no time to make dinner. I later found out my wife's grandmother always spoiled any pup with a hamburger to make instant friends. Coincidence? I think not. Floppy went to the end of the kitchen and lay down. No begging, just contentment. Strange for a shelter dog and grandma was impressed. Floppy passed. He got a burger.

That night in bed I told my wife I'd always wanted a dog named Bear. When I raced SuperCross, my bike mechanic and sponsor had a large Lab by that name who greeted me after each race, his tail whipping back and forth, with wet kisses to follow. That dog just stuck with me all these years. My wife gave her approval and Floppy officially became Bear. When he lay down next to our bed for his first night, letting out a deep growling sigh, I knew I had a new companion and he'd found a forever home.

One potty on the floor and a potty in the garage, because of confusion most likely, were the only times he had an accident. Bear must have been potty trained. Although our daughters blamed him once for pooping in their pool, it was their little sister. Sit, shake, come, roll over, were all natural to our Bear. Why would someone let go of this fine dog after training him?

Eventually, we noticed his legs shook uncontrollably and at times, he could barely stand. At his first vet visit, our vet explained that many people get large dogs, but don't have room for them. The dogs are housed in crates and never get the exercise needed to build strength in their legs, which atrophy. Bear got a clean bill of health other than his legs. Next came shots and neutering, poor guy. Maybe that's why we related to each other so well. Let's just say my wife and I won't be having any more children. I'm glad I didn't have to wear a cone around my neck.

Flowers and gardens were a place of comfort for Bear, who loved to dig and play. We didn't scold him, but instead took pictures of a happy dog and three mischievous little girls. That summer flew faster than the dragonflies zipping past our heads on late August evenings. Bear loved to chase them, as well as bees, which cost him a swollen tongue and a trip to the doggy ER for a shot to counteract the allergic reaction.

One late August day started just like the day before. "Take good care of them while I'm at work," I said to Bear, with a pat to his head as I went out the door. When I arrived at work, the air was heavy and thick, with less blue than usual in the sky. Was that a sign? Maybe. The crew was eager to get a test started, as a big client was waiting on results of its newest underwater meter that would measure oil and gas flow from wells deep in the ocean floor. As health and safety administrator and flow technician, I was to oversee proper installation of the experiment into our test loop.

My gut told me that something was wrong, and I told the crew leader I was thinking of quitting. "If you quit, we all quit," he said. I couldn't allow that. I couldn't let them down. We began the test.

Suddenly, the lifting straps shock loaded or slipped, causing 2 1/2 tons of piping and our client's meter to shift and fall. It stopped short of the ground, but a bolt caught my right arm, and my life changed forever. I just didn't know it yet.

When I tried to pull my arm out, a flash of blue and white shot through my mind, as pain spread down my neck and back. My arm had nearly been ripped from its socket. Pain shot into my right hip too, as I balanced on metal 25 feet above the ground. The equipment survived well, but my body didn't. When I got home from the hospital, I knew I'd never work again. Suddenly, I was caught in a system of doctors and insurance battles, with no end. Depression washed over me as I took a pill for this and a pill for that. The pills became my meals, or at least seemed to be. I was unable to provide for my family, play with my kids, or even cut my own food.

Bear seemed to like having me at home, even if I couldn't throw a ball or go for walks. He became my shoulder to cry on when I felt shut out. He became my nurse when my breathing became shallow from the painkillers, giving me a gentle nudge to bring me back from the dark. He took over my role as the alpha of the house.

He barked only for good cause, and greeted people at the door with a sniff of their butts. "That's how dogs shake hands," I told everyone. His sense of smell was one of his most impressive traits. Glove lost in four feet of Colorado powder? Bear could find it. Maybe his calling was to be a search and rescue dog serving high in the Rocky Mountains. Or perhaps he would have been at home on a tennis court. He loved those yellow balls, and always had one in mouth, even when eating.

With his own chair and plate at the table, Bear didn't need to beg. Instead, 100 pounds of love would stare at me, waiting for the words, "Time to eat!"

He was good to the cats— and we had plenty of them, including 28 foster cats, 20 of whom were kittens. We brought them home because my wife wanted to help the shelter where we got Bear the

year before. My only complaint was they taught Bear how to be a cat, and then he was on the table, with his furry, feline friends.

My condition continued to worsen. My wife's little brother moved in to help her with the kids and her biggest baby, me. Aaron took Bear for walks, rollerbladed with Bear around our park, and played fetch for hours. For Bear this was great, but he needed a canine friend. From the shelter, we adopted Nika, a black and white, blue-eyed, husky. They had just one fight . . . on the first date. Nika established herself as the alpha, Bear showed his belly, they sniffed butts and became inseparable. Isn't that how love works?

Seven years passed, and it was the week before Christmas. Our girls were home for winter break and excitement filled the air. Since Christmas for dogs comes only once every seven years, we always made it special for them. This year was no different, with balls, bones, pull ropes, and squeaky toys in their stockings.

Nika wanted out for her last potty break of the evening. As she walked our fence line she acted strange. Bear went to take a look and she nipped at him. I called for her to come, but her back legs wouldn't work and she started to whine and whimper. After struggling to get her into the house, my wife and her brother got her to the kitchen, where she collapsed. Then we placed her on a blanket and loaded her into my truck. Her kidneys had failed, the vet told us. She had to be put down. The next day my father and his helper used pickaxes to dig her grave in the frozen ground for me and placed her among the graves of other beloved family pets. I kept her collar and tags.

When I got home, Bear was sleeping at the very spot his love had fallen in the kitchen the night before. The sound of her tags brought him to his feet and a frantic search ensued, running through the house and out the door to check the fence line. Bear then came to me with a lost look, and I could see his heart was broken. I put Nika's collar and tags in my toolbox. I couldn't bear to hear the sound either. Together we sat on the step and cried.

As my thoughts became darker, so did Bear's. Separation anxiety came daily for him, as he was lost without Nika and I was now forced to make more trips to the doctor. I had to keep an eye on a lump and look for blood in my stool and vomit. I knew before anyone things were not right, but I continued to hold out hope. Just touching my skin hurt. My gut spoke again, "Something's wrong."

A phone call from the doctor took my breath away. "I'm sorry, but I think it's cancer," he said. I tried to hang up the phone, but it slid from my trembling hand and I started to cry. I told my wife the news. Our world stopped again. Was it stomach cancer? Why now, and why us?

Bear looked at the ceiling and back at me. "If I cut a hole here and put the rope there, all I need is for that ladder to move itself. It will be over quick," I thought.

But it isn't easy for a guy to tie a noose when he can't tie his own shoes. "Scratch that idea," I told Bear. Pills and alcohol seemed simpler. Bear sat through my tangents and tirades, and eight months of prescription drug withdrawals. Everyone told me not to think about the unthinkable. "Think of your kids, your wife and what you have to give the world," they said. Strange thing was, I knew my wife and kids would be taken care of. But what about Bear? Would the next guy talk to him the way we talked? Would he get in trouble for being on the furniture or snuggling in bed? What about Christmas?

Miraculously, I got the all clear on my cancer scare. I had a nuclear disease with leaky stomach syndrome and the acid had entered my lymph nodes. The pills had not been good to me. I lost 100 pounds in three months. Both Bear and I now had gray hair and he had a dry and cracked nose. We had aged considerably during the past 4,000 days together, and another Colorado spring was just around the corner.

It was 3 a.m. and Bear became restless, needing out to do his business. I had just let him out not an hour before. A trip to the vet the next morning brought unexpected and devastating news. "I'm sorry but Bear has a tumor the size of a grapefruit blocking his intestinal tract. Surgery is an option but he's at stage 4. I give him two weeks to two months. The steroids and pain killers will help only for awhile," the vet said.

As I loaded Bear into my truck, tears filled my eyes and I could barely see to drive us the five blocks home. "I'm sorry," I told my daughters, who were awaiting the news. "We'll do everything we can to make him comfortable."

Bear's last snow had melted, tulip bulbs were just breaking ground when I sat and had my last talk with him. "Old man, you've been good to me. I hope you can say the same about me. I love you and I wish I could do more."

Bear turned and looked away, maybe so I couldn't see his tears. I know he saw mine. My family gathered in the garage and huddled around our old Bear. I went to my tool box and picked up Nika's collar and tags I'd placed there so many years before. Bear lifted his head from his bed and looked around, sniffing her last scent. I placed her collar around his neck. He seemed happy to have her with him again.

My wife and I drove him around town for one last ride, and then we met our girls at the vet's office. We all surrounded Bear, petting and talking to him as the muscle relaxer was injected. His eyes drew heavy as I lay next to him on the floor, clutching him in my arms.

"Are you ready for the last injection?" the vet asked." I nodded my head and whispered in his ear, "I love you buddy. Go play with Nika."

14. Party Animals
By Sammie Justesen

The author is a registered nurse, artist, publisher, and former president of the Rowan County Humane Society. She managed a no-kill animal shelter for several years and continues to love and foster animals. She grew up on a farm in southern Indiana and has returned home after many years of wandering.

When we moved to the mountains of eastern Kentucky, my husband Bob and I never considered owning a dog, although we shared our home with several cats and half a dozen guinea pigs. But the moment I saw the litter of pups born to our neighbor's Alaskan husky, I fell in love. The mother was a purebred who came under the spell of a Kentucky "yeller dog" chained in the backyard next to our house. About 60 days later, she gave birth to 10 adorable pups. The friendliest pup in the litter soon joined our family and we named him Beaudreau, or Beau (pronounced Boo), because the name fit his Cajun-like personality. Beau resembled his mom, with classic black-tan-white husky markings and a tail that curled over his back like a flag. He could smile and loved to play the clown.

Beaudreau

Later we would discover his uncanny homing instinct. After we moved to a new house, Beau periodically returned to the "old home place" to visit his mom. By coincidence (or not), his first visit happened on Mother's Day. When we received a phone call and came to pick up Beau, he was gone. We feared the worst, knowing he would have to cover many miles, find his way over a forest-covered mountain, and cross a busy highway to get home. No worries—he showed up an hour later, cheerful and a bit tired. After a few more episodes, we realized we could turn him loose anywhere and he'd come home.

When Beau was about six months old, Bob returned from a trip to Minnesota with a surprise for me—a puppy. This plump little guy resulted from another breeding mishap—his father a full blooded Newfoundland and the mother a registered Tervuren (Belgian shepherd). We named him Amos. Beau was jealous of the new arrival, but smart enough not to show it. He would "accidently" bump the

Amos

pup and knock him over. During a walk in the woods I caught Beau trying to roll Amos off the side of a cliff. When I shouted, "Beau, NO!"he looked at me with innocent eyes, as if to say, "I was just trying to help him. He tripped."

Fortunately, Amos grew fast and within a few months exceeded 100 pounds, with long, silky black fur, webbed feet from his Newfie father, and (fortunately) no drooling. Amos had a mellow disposition; calm and loyal to us, and less exuberant than Beau. Amos in the Bible was the prophet of righteousness, and our Amos would turn out to be a fair and just pack leader.

But we didn't have a pack—yet. When Beau and Amos were about a year old, a neighbor begged us to adopt the full blooded Siberian husky he could no longer care for. Aptly named Wolf, this fierce looking dog had an incredibly thick coat, a curly tail, and one blue eye. He did resemble a wolf, which intimidated people who didn't know about his gentle nature around humans. Wolf definitely came equipped

Wolf

for a Siberian winter. Invigorated by cold weather, he and Beau loved playing in the snow and I wished we had a dog sled for them to pull.

Amos became the pack leader after a week or so of half-serious fights with Wolf. The three dogs were neutered, which helped reduce their aggression. Beau wanted to be the leader, but did not have the temperament. Wolf *seriously* wanted the job, but Amos could—and would—throw Wolf to the ground and stand over him. About once a month Wolf tested Amos with a play fight that always ended with the same result: Wolf on his back. Amos became a fine leader, showing wisdom and patience in all things.

Now, we had a dog pack, totally unplanned, and three large canine friends who needed to run, and run, and run—especially the huskies. Fortunately, our property bordered the Daniel Boone

National Forest, which includes some of the most rugged terrain west of the Appalachian Mountains and covers more than 700,000 acres. Perfect for dogs. Every day, rain or shine, I climbed the mountain behind our house with the dogs. Those were among the best evenings of my life as I followed behind The Pack, listening to them yip as they charged through the woods. If they flushed game, the huskies would run for miles before coming back to me. I meandered along the trails, noting signs of the changing seasons, scat from wildlife, and the abundant small critters—snakes, lizards, box turtles, chipmunks, squirrels, and so on. Amos often stayed at my side and we perched atop a huge rock where I could watch the world below us while running my fingers through his silky fur. He would give a contented sigh and close his eyes. Let the huskies have their fun—he enjoyed my companionship. Sometimes my tabby cat came with us, trailing the pack up the mountain or riding across my shoulders.

The dogs loved meeting people and never showed signs of aggression—until Amos grew older. With maturity, we realized he had protective genes from both the Belgian shepherd and the Newfoundland side of his heritage. I discovered this for sure one weekend when he travelled with us for an overnight hotel stay in Lexington. I had taken him outside on a leash and was heading back to the room when a nice looking man started a conversation about the weather. As I answered him, Amos lunged at the man, snarling, with fangs bared. The poor guy ran down the hallway and I shouted an apology, hoping he wouldn't call the front desk. On the elevator, another man spoke to me and Amos did the same thing. I soon realized my dog had set a new standard: I was not allowed to talk to other men when Bob wasn't with us. Sheesh. Suddenly, I had a large, hairy chaperone with strict rules and zero tolerance. No flirting for me.

The next incident occurred when a policeman pulled Bob over for a traffic stop, with Amos in the front seat of the truck. The officer spoke harshly. With no warning, Amos lunged across Bob's lap and almost grabbed an arm through the window. Luckily the cop had quick reflexes and Bob pulled Amos away. Attacking a Kentucky State Trooper was not good.

The officer shouted, "You control that dog or I'm going to shoot it!" Bob carefully slid out of the truck to accept his speeding ticket. Later, we learned this trooper had a reputation for being arrogant and hostile with the public. When word spread about the traffic stop, Amos developed a cult following among local rednecks. He was welcome in every liquor store and bar in the county.

His reputation grew even more after a second event.

In the evenings, Bob like to hang out at a general store where local guys congregated to drink beer and talk guy stuff. Amos had a reserved sleeping spot behind the counter. One night Amos was asleep, seemingly heedless of his surroundings, when a man entered the store. Bob said later, "He looked like a perfectly ordinary feller to me."

Within seconds Amos emitted a war cry and charged the guy, teeth bared like a grizzly bear. The man's face drained of color. He ran backward, stumbled out the door, and scrambled into his truck. Amos stayed at the door, growling until the taillights disappeared.

Bob could hardly believe his eyes. "I don't know what got into Amos," he told the owner. "I'm real sorry."

"I know what got into him," the storekeeper said. "That man just got out of jail for armed robbery—holding up liquor stores. He's mean as a snake, and I didn't want him in my place. I have no doubt he was up to no good when he came in here tonight. That dog is a hero."

Amos ate two packs of Slim Jims and went back to sleep.

Around this time I joined the local Humane Society, which had five stalwart members. At my first meeting they convinced me to be president, because everyone else had already tried the job. We all volunteered at the county dog shelter—a depressing cement block building located miles out of town near the water treatment plant. The entire area reeked of dog poop and the so-called shelter was damp, cold, and cheerless. Healthy dogs were euthanized weekly and seldom adopted. In fact, the animal control officer sometimes shot dogs and buried them nearby so he wouldn't have to drive them into town for euthanization at the vet's office.

These conditions broke my heart. I took photos and made a presentation for the judge executive, who ran the county with a firm hand. Rather than confront him, which the other members had tried without success, I entered his office with a more humble attitude: "The shelter is a mess, and I know the animal control officer is struggling. I think we can make things better if we work together instead of arguing."

The judge liked my approach. In fact, he approved of it so much that he called my cell phone an hour later and said, "How would you like to take over running the shelter?"

Yikes! Be careful what you wish for. The six of us took over the rundown shelter with a 30-dog capacity, 1.5 employees, and a tight budget. None of us were paid. Our first order of business was to make it a no-kill facility. This added to our challenges, but we couldn't bear to see another healthy dog put down.

My *real* job was homecare RN for the local hospital. My area included the shelter and my boss loved dogs—thank goodness. I could stop on my lunch break to check on things and feed the animals. Somehow, with teamwork, struggles, and occasional frustration, we made things work and gained public support for the dog shelter. Walmart gave us dog food, allowed us to hold adoption events inside the store, and let us place photos of dogs on a bulletin board seen by half the people in the county.

When certain animals needed special care in order to survive, several of us opened our homes to foster dogs, after having them checked by our vet. When I began bringing home dogs, The Pack took on a new role. On a typical day, I would unload the newcomer from the back seat of my car and show her around the house and yard. The dog would have her own private space in the garage with a warm bed, a food dish, and fresh water. I'd leave her alone for a while to settle. Later, she would come out on a leash to meet the other dogs. I quickly learned to let Amos handle this delicate moment. He would sniff the newbie from head to tail while the rest of us watched. Some shelter dogs cowered on the ground. Others rolled onto their backs in submission. Many trembled in fear, but Amos never showed aggression unless provoked.

When Amos wagged his tail, the new dog was "in." Wolf sometimes got pushy because he was sensitive and jealous of his second-in-command status. Amos would watch these interactions and intervene as needed. No bullying was allowed on his watch, and one growl from Amos made Wolfie stand down.

I brought home a young female Rottweiler named Hope whose severely bowed legs barely supported her. She suffered from rickets caused by cheap food and malnutrition. Her hair was rough and patchy, her eyes dull and sad. The vet wasn't sure she'd make it, and we agreed she would die in the dog shelter. So she came home with me, where Amos, Beau, and Wolf treated her like a queen. With love, security, and good food, she regained her health and became a happy, active, glossy-haired dog. I posted before-and-after photos at Walmart, and soon an eight-year- old girl and her mom became Hope's new owners.

While driving to a home health visit deep in the mountains, I spotted two puppies someone had dumped with a load of garbage. I caught the first pup right away, but his sister ran from me and I spent two hours coaxing her out of hiding. Puppies didn't do well at the shelter, so I brought them home to The Pack for socialization. Again, the boys showed great tenderness and before long I found the pups a good home where they could stay together.

One afternoon, a starving, dehydrated, filthy coonhound burst from the woods and ran behind my car on top of Clack Mountain. Luckily, I saw him in the rear view mirror and stopped. Festus (the name I instantly gave him) was so happy to be rescued, he jumped all over me. He smelled horrible and spread muck on my clothes and the back seat of the car. Later, a kind hunter adopted him.

And so it continued over the years. Our three special dogs became mentors for dozens of homeless canines, and even cats. Some of the strays were injured, starved, frightened, and recovering from illness, but The Pack showed them how good life could be. All dogs lived well at our place.

Speaking of the good life . . . We built racks for the back of Bob's truck and sometimes took The Pack to walk on the fire trails in other sections of the national forest. On one memorable fall evening we walked for almost an hour, encountering a five-foot timber rattler, wild turkeys, and various other wildlife. The dogs flushed a deer and charged into the deep woods, as usual. But this time something was different: They did not come back. We heard gunshots in the distance. This worried us, because we knew the local marijuana growers—some of them returned combat soldiers—set up compounds on public land and guarded their crops with bobby traps and guns. We didn't think they'd shoot our dogs, but who knew?

We called and whistled, again and again. At dusk we walked back to the trailhead and waited at the truck. Still no dogs. By that time Bob was cursing the dogs, their parents, and every canine who ever drew breath. This was the Friday of Labor Day weekend, and as the sun set over the mountains, vehicles filled with college kids began arriving. Three guys gathered wood for a fire, while others unloaded coolers and kegs.

"What's up?" We asked.

"Big party and bonfire all night," one of the guys answered. "You're welcome to stay." We were a bit long of tooth for a college kegger, but we wished them well. After much discussion we drove home, got the car, and returned with both vehicles. We decided to leave our truck beside the trail and hope the dogs would stay with it, if they came back. The boys promised to watch for them, but I had to wonder if anyone would be sober enough to remember that promise. I told myself Beau could always find his way home, but not if something happened to him or one of the other dogs.

I lay awake most of the night creating morbid scenarios: 1) The dogs were injured or killed by bears, coyotes, rattlesnakes, or pot growers; 2) the dogs arrived at the party, freaked out, and ran away for good; or 3) the dogs went home with college kids and ended up joining a fraternity.

Early the next morning we returned to the trail and called for The Pack. A mound of embers smoldered in the fire pit and a few sleepy looking kids were picking up trash. No dogs in sight.

"Oh, no," I breathed. "They're really gone."

"Did you see three dogs last night?" Bob asked one of the guys.

I held my breath as the young man frowned and stared into the distance. "Dogs? Oh, yeah. We had three big dogs here. They were great. Stayed for the whole party and had hot dogs and beer. They were a big hit."

"Do you know where they went?" I asked.

He shrugged. "No idea. Sorry."

Bob turned away to hide his tears, muttering under his breath. For him, anger and sadness often mingled.

I heaved a gigantic sigh. What should we do next? I could walk the trail again and blow a whistle. Thinking hard, I headed for the truck to get my hat from the front seat. And there, sprawled in the truck bed, lay the three dogs, snoring and hung over. Their breath reeked of beer and hot dogs. Wolf looked up at me, burped, and closed his eyes. They barely roused when we raised the tailgate and drove home. The party animals slept all day, and then drank gallons of water before wandering into the living room that evening.

"Great party! What's next?" They seemed to say. "Let's go back!"

"You dogs are turning my hair gray," I told them as I lowered myself to the floor and let the three of them lean against me. "No more parties."

We enjoyed many more adventures and 10 amazing years with The Pack. But, alas, we humans usually outlive our dogs. Beau was first to go, then Wolfie, and finally our beloved Amos. I can't even write about them without shedding tears. I try and remember the words of a six-year-old boy named Shane, whose elderly dog had to be put down. When his parents wondered aloud why animal lives have to be shorter than human lives, Shane said, "I know why."

Startled, they turned to him. He said, "People are born so that they can learn how to live a good life—like loving everybody all the time and being nice, right?" He continued, "Well, dogs already know how to do that, so they don't have to stay as long."

Thank you, guys, for all the wonderful years. I know I'll see you again in Heaven.

PART THREE: My Best Friend

15. Pippa Is Still Gone

Also a rescue dog, Ursa, a Lab-Rhodesian ridgeback mix, was the most laid back dog that I'd ever owned and one of the most mellow I'd ever seen. I could run a vacuum cleaner over her back or belly and she wouldn't budge. She didn't open an eye when thunder cracked. And she totally ignored distant gunshots during hunting season, as well as the barrage of fireworks that assaulted my rural community for two or three weeks surrounding the 4th of July.

Pippa was the polar opposite. And because the difference was so stark, it caught me off guard when a spring thunder boomer started her quaking and shaking, before fleeing into the bathroom.

As I thought about this, it made sense that she would be afraid. Spending her first two years of life in a shelter, she hadn't seen, smelled, or experienced much of life. She hadn't heard much of it either, at least not in a natural setting. Her entire life had been overlaid by the smells, sights, and sounds of the shelter, and two dozen or so other dogs, most of whom were quick to bark, howl, and whine at the least provocation.

Growing up in a home, a pup is more likely to hear noises in their purer form, and, consequently, accept them as part of everyday life. To help that along, many hunters gradually introduce their young dogs to loud noises on a regular basis so they won't be frightened by gunshots in the field.

Some dogs, though, are afflicted with noise anxiety no matter how they were raised. Experts estimate that 15 million or more dogs suffer with it. The general belief is that some are more susceptible than others, with herding breeds such as collies and shepherds among the mostly likely victims. I intentionally don't know Pippa's DNA mix. I prefer the mystery. But she certainly could have herding breed genes, considering her build, speed, and agility.

For Pippa, then, it could be a double whammy. But whatever the reasons, loud noises, especially those with a concussive component, sent her into blind panic. I quickly learned after I brought her home from the shelter that it manifested with an ominous pause in which all reason seemed to leave her body and fear radiated from her eyes. Then she ran. In the house that wasn't such a problem because her options were limited. During the first couple of months of spring thunderstorms, she darted from room to room, panting and shaking. What I came to realize was that she seemed to reason she could escape by going from where she was to someplace else. Of course, she couldn't. Eventually she decided to hide in the darkest recesses of the guest bathroom, although I thought under the stairs in the basement would be her preferred refuge.

Storm jackets or thunder shirts, intended to reduce anxiety by constantly applying gentle pressure to the torso, did nothing for Pippa, although they are reputed in help with more than 75 percent of afflicted pets. And a sedative prescribed by the veterinarian was useful only inside, for obvious reasons, and then only when given well in advance of thunder or celebratory explosions.

Outside, I realized, I must be prudent and keep her on a leash during certain times, such as when the sky showed signs of an approaching storm, or around the 4th of July, when people were most likely to set off fireworks.

Allowing her off the leash early in the morning during 4th of July weekend for a brief frolic in the water didn't seem unreasonable.

But that decision had catastrophic consequences. One firecracker panicked her. And just as I was coaxing her within reach, a second explosion sent her running. Inside, she would have retreated to the darkened bathroom. Outside, though, she had no refuge. By the time she stopped running in search of a safe place, she was long gone.

As the day progressed, kids would light more firecrackers, with each explosion heightening her fear. And evening in this area would be Hell on Earth for a dog with noise anxiety, as the orchestrated pyrotechnics commenced. By morning, she would be far away from me or dead on the highway, struck as she tried to cross in blind panic.

"Pippa! Pippa!" I screamed and chased after her, as the second firecracker sent her sprinting away. "Pippa!"

I ran and called and ran until I could no longer see her.

For most of three days and nights, I played that life-changing moment over and over in my mind. Of course, I did other things too, most of them directed at finding her, even though my rational mind told me the chances were slim to none.

*   *   *   *   *

First, I had to get home. The lake was a mile from my house, and I was on foot. I called for Pippa as I jogged. A friend who also walked his dog every morning told me that he'd seen her run by and called to her. Normally, she would have responded, because Pippa liked both my friend and his dog, but this time she ignored him. At least he could give me the direction she was going.

As I learned later, Pippa ran two miles, where someone at a convenience store somehow managed to get his hands on her. He attached her collar to a newspaper vending machine and went inside. I never learned what he did in the store or what he intended to do with Pippa when he came back outside. It didn't matter.

She wiggled out of her collar and took off again. Now, even if someone else did find Pippa, that person would have no way of identifying her or knowing that she belonged to me. That realization, piled on top of my guilt and the constant replay of what happened at the lake, made it difficult for me to press on. But I did.

I checked out our normal walking routes, vainly hoping to find my lost companion. I drove for miles and miles in a circle around the area, pausing frequently to call her name. When I saw people walking or working in their yards, I stopped and asked if they'd seen her. I prayed. Sometimes late at night, when I wasn't strong enough and visualized the worst, I cried.

Fortunately, I also called the Farmington Pet Adoption Center, and the kind folks there advised that I post her photo and information on my Facebook page and share it to theirs. I did.

On the morning of the third day I got a hit, although the news was a mixed blessing. Someone had seen a dog matching Pippa's appearance, a medium-size black dog with white toes and white chest blaze, going through her garbage. If that was her, Pippa was still alive. But she was even farther away.

Then came the phone call that I was certain never would come but, somehow, miraculously did. Damien Bell was confident the dog that his father, Billy, found on his property in an adjacent county was Pippa.

On the second day of Pippa's disappearance, Billy's dogs alerted him that something was hiding under one of his sheds. "Dad went up to see what all the commotion was about," Damien later told me. "He penned up all of the dogs and then tried to coax her out. It took him about an hour.

"Once he could reach her, he grabbed her and put a collar and lead on her. He had Mom release the other dogs from their fenced-in back yard and put her in there."

Later, simply as a joke, Damien's wife, Sarah, texted him to ask if any new dogs had shown up at his parents' home. "It seems like every dog in Missouri finds its way to their house," he explained.

Yes, one had. When Damien described the dog to Sarah, she recognized it from my Facebook posts and he called me.

I was afraid to believe it was true. I was afraid to believe that somehow, someway, Pippa had traveled at least 10 miles along both a busy county road and a highway, to find her way to the home of someone kind enough to catch and care for a shy, frightened dog with no collar. Damien assured me it was her.

Later that day, the Bell family met me at the convenience store to return Pippa to me. Of course, I was overjoyed. Pippa was not. In fact, she was so unresponsive that I feared her rescuers might suspect she wasn't really mine. But we moved her from their vehicle to mine without incident, and they followed me home.

I learned that Damien loved fishing as much as I, and giving him a couple of my books on the subject was the least that I could do. More than three years later, we still say in touch, and I will be forever grateful to him and his family for their generosity.

And four years later, Pippa and I have bonded. What I hadn't realized until the Bells returned her to me was that four months weren't long enough for that to happen. A dog who has been alone in a crowd, with no real companionship for its first two years of life, needs time. For me, that wasn't a negative. It was simply reality, and despite this near tragedy, made me even more confident I'd done the right thing in adopting an adult dog. Puppies are easy to love and usually quick to be adopted. Adults not so much, and yet they have so much to offer in return. Pippa is sweet, obedient, quick to learn, eager to please, and a loyal, loving companion. These fine qualities far overshadow her fear, shyness, discomfort around strangers, and a desire to be by herself from time to time, especially at night.

Today, when Pippa is frightened by a noise, or anything else, she comes to me and leans against my leg in much the same way she did on the first day that I met her. With a long nose that can knock your elbow sideways, she seeks out affection instead of just accepting it. Each and every morning, she's extraordinarily happy as she greets me, eager to go on our morning walk, chase squirrels, play in the water, and inhale deeply of the world's many splendiferous odors.

What I did notice on that day more than three years ago, was that Pippa did seem happy to be "home." Although she didn't acknowledge me as someone special when I picked her up at the convenience store, she quickly relaxed inside, didn't try to hide, and even positioned her head under my hand so she could be petted. Acquiring a desire for affection took less time to grow than developing a bond with me.

Knowing what made her exquisitely happy, I decided to give her a welcome-home treat. Under a late afternoon sun, I took her back out in the front yard and turned her loose. At the shelter, she spent most of her life on pavement or gravel, her feet touching natural ground only on brief walks. Now, tongue lolling, eyes rolling, she moaned in delight as she wiggled and squirmed in the lush green grass.

I laughed, as I always do while watching this celebration of pure, unadulterated happiness. Only this time, tears stained my cheeks as I gave silent thanks for the miracle of Pippa's return.

16. Do I Know You?

"The greatest fear dogs know is the fear that you will not come back when you go out the door without them."

—*Stanley Coren*

A s I drive away from the boarding kennel with Pippa in the back seat, this is the conversation that I imagine taking place around the front desk of the facility:

Receptionist: "Did you see that? He was gone for a week and she wasn't happy to see him."

Assistant: "I know. It was like he was a complete stranger. I wonder if he beats her."

Receptionist: "Poor thing! What an awful man!"

Of course, I never beat Pippa. I would never hurt her in any way. Discipline consists of my "mean voice," which I used to great effect when I was a teacher, combined with putting her on a leash when she doesn't respond immediately for my call to return. This works for awhile, until she's struck with another round of deafness while standing under an oak tree, trying to determine where a squirrel went.

Our relationship is about love and affection 99.9 percent of the time.

Then what the hell is going on when I pick her up at the boarding kennel after returning from a trip? Every time this happens, I am sorely tempted to say, "I don't know why Pippa does this. I really don't." But people who feel guilt tend to talk too much and over-explain. And I'm not one of them. Well, okay, I am a little bit. Maybe other dogs respond to their masters' return in the same way that Pippa does. Or, more accurately, don't respond.

I look in the rearview mirror to check if Pippa has a doggy smirk on her face, knowing she played a trick on me. But she's lying comfortably in the back seat, head on her front paws, eyes closed, and not a smirk to be seen. She lazily opens one brown eye and we exchange glances in the mirror. "Ha! Ha!" her twinkling gaze seems to say. Or maybe it's just my imagination.

But why does she do it?

Ursa, her predecessor, wasn't that way. As with "normal"dogs separated from their masters, she was always jubilant when I picked her up. Her backside contorted wildly as she whined with joy and licked my face.

Except for the kisses, Daisy, a friend's black Lab, greeted me with similar excitement when we visited a couple of times a week. First, she announced our arrival with her distinctive jubilant bark. Then she whined and snaked around and between my legs, before flopping down on her back for a belly rub.

Down in Florida, meanwhile, BB, a black Pekapoo owned by a fishing buddy, dances and prances and cries with seeming ecstasy when I arrive for my annual visit. And each morning I'm there, she hurries back to the guest room to greet me with nearly the same enthusiasm she shows upon my arrival. Each morning she wants to hurry me into the kitchen to be with her and her master, as if she knows I'm there for a limited time and she wants to make every minute count. Remember Lassie leading the search party to rescue Timmy from the well? It's a lot like that.

Some scientists believe dogs show greater affection toward their owners (and friends) if they've been separated for longer periods of time. "As the amount of time away increases, so does the dogs' excitement," reports the *Animal Planet* website. "This will come as no surprise to dog owners; most canines get excited about the return of the master to the castle, especially after long absences. But this research is also important because it shows dogs are capable of recognizing and responding to different spans of time."

Tell that to Pippa. Whether my trip was brief or long doesn't matter. Someone leads her to the front desk and hands the leash to me. Pippa dutifully sits and accepts my greeting, hugs, and strokes with a figurative yawn. Occasionally, her tail might brush once or twice across the floor. At least she doesn't cringe and try to escape, which might prompt someone to call Animal Protective Services, if such an agency existed.

The first time this happened, I thought nothing of it. After all, she spent her first two years in a kennel. But it has continued for more than three years now, and I'm starting to develop a complex.

I do have a couple of theories:

While Pippa is the happiest and most energetic dog I've ever seen when she's running free, she instantly becomes docile and submissive when placed on a leash. She was that way when I first met her, and remains that way today. This behavior appears to be something she does naturally, so I can't take credit for it. When we're approaching traffic, houses, and/or strangers, I call her to me. She responds promptly and we continue on our way, with her by my side. I see other people being dragged around by their dogs and think how lucky I am—except when Pippa embarrasses me at the kennel. Perhaps the leash explains her passivity.

Another possibility relates to the fact that we've bonded, although it took awhile because of her history. I noticed her recognizing and being happy to return "home" before I saw her relating to me as someone special. Behavior experts believe some shelter dogs are capable of bonding within a half-hour of meeting someone because they want a home so badly. Pippa hasn't proven to be one of them.

Now, I have no doubt that we are bonded, and it was worth the wait. I see the saddest aspect of that when I drop her off at the kennel. She doesn't want me to leave without her. On the other hand, happy-go-lucky Ursa didn't seem to mind at all. She could nap, enjoy treats, and revel in the affection showered upon her by employees who said she was their favorite. One even told me that she was taking a photo of Ursa with her when she went back to college.

I also see that Pippa and I have bonded when we're visiting a friend. If I get up to go to the bathroom, Pippa goes with me. If we let her out onto his deck she won't leave it, even though several oh-so-tempting squirrels scurry around below.

I see it when we play. The friskier I get, the friskier she gets. And when I'm silent in the morning, so is she. Although she loves our morning walks, she shows no eagerness at all until I sit down to put on my shoes and call her. Then I take her head in my hands, rub her ears, and ask her if she's ready. Of course she is! And with the permission provided to her by my voice and actions, she shows it.

Possibly if I showed more enthusiasm when I picked her up at the kennel, she would as well. Or maybe I'd just look like more of a fool because the leash is the key. Or Pippa is having fun at my expense as retribution for leaving her there.

But, seriously, I am not one to attribute such motives to dogs. I think people who rationalize their pets' negative behavior by attaching human emotions such as revenge, anger, and jealousy are wrong. When dogs act inappropriately, the behavior is a response to stress or anxiety instead of a desire to lash out at someone to whom they are unconditionally devoted.

Bottom line, I think Pippa never will behave as a "normal" dog in some situations. My two theories probably have merit, but the biggest factor for Pippa was spending her first two years—the equivalent of 14 human years—in confinement. Although she was around people who fed and cared for her, she didn't bond with them. She never learned to play. She had no opportunity to socialize or explore life outside the kennel. Even now sometimes, when she comes to me for affection, she maintains a small separation between us and I must lean in to reach her. As I do, I'm reminded of a child on the autism spectrum. When we come in from our afternoon/evening walk, Pippa often chooses to stay alone in the basement until the next morning.

Yet, by so many other actions and gestures, I know she loves me as much as I love her.

"Our dogs are always willing to undertake joint actions with us, to master rules of behavior, and, if the circumstances demand, to defend or serve us without regard to their own interests," said Vilmos Csanyi, an animal behavior expert and author of the book *If Dogs Could Talk.* "A dog and a master who have grown used to each other truly behave like a unit in a joint activity."

That definitely describes Pippa and me when we walk. For example, when we come to an intersection, usually with her well in front, she will pause. I then direct her by both voice and gesture which way we're going and she immediately responds. Occasionally, she charges too far ahead and I must call her back. Usually she's self-regulating and will either wait for her slower master or come running back to me and then sprint forward again. As I often tell friends, "I walk three miles a day with Pippa, and she runs six."

Also, if I am picking up twigs to use as kindling in the fireplace, Pippa often will mimic the action. She thinks it's play time. She'll grab a stick, run, and then lie down with it several yards away. When I approach, her butt goes up in the air, she chomps down on the stick, and her brown eyes flash with the joy of being alive. Then she takes off again.

Considering all the love and pleasure Pippa provides otherwise, I guess I should just learn to live with embarrassment I feel each time we leave the boarding kennel. Still, I keep glancing in that rearview mirror—just in case.

17. Doggy Style

"Butts are to dogs as bacon is to humans."

— Unknown

*A*romatically speaking, they're irresistible. That's what Pippa told me.

Although I believe she's a canine Einstein, she has not yet mastered the English language. She revealed her opinion not in words, but by sniffing the butt of a life-size statue of her buddy Daisy, who died awhile back. A bit startled by the sudden appearance of the replica on my friend Bob's patio, she circled it carefully and then went straight for the concrete bottom. On subsequent visits, she did the same thing, although not quite so enthusiastically. Even now, months later, she occasionally pauses to give the faux Daisy an olfactory inspection.

This butt-sniffing was the same protocol they followed each time they met. Why did they bother? It wasn't as if they didn't know each other by sight. Why not just get down to the business of playing or running down to the lake, where Daisy barked at fish and ducks and Pippa watched?

You could say it's the canine equivalent of saying "hello," but it's much more than that. As we depend primarily on our eyes to relate to the world, dogs depend on their noses, which are up to

100,000 times more sensitive than ours. About one third of their brain mass is devoted to detecting and identifying odors, while we utilize just five percent.

When people meet, we subconsciously notice body language, facial expressions, and tone of voice. These cues help us determine whether we should shake hands, share a hug, or simply say "Hi."

Dogs typically circle and gauge one another's posture and attitude. Are the ears back? Is the tail wagging? Are hackles raised? Following this visual assessment, they head straight for the butt, whether the other canine is friend or a stranger, to get a whiff of the anal glands or sacs. Chemical secreted by these glands help dogs get acquainted or renew friendships. They reveal gender, diet, emotional state, and many other things we humans, with our less developed sense of smell, can only imagine.

And, yes, the farther the nose goes up there, the more information is received. Call it the canine equivalent of "brown nosing," although with a more forthright intent.

"Mutual rear-sniffing is the most natural thing in the world when you're a dog," said Jeff Stallings, a certified professional dog trainer and behavior consultant." You have to remember that the dogs' sense of smell is roughly equivalent to our sense of sight. With over 300 million olfactory receptor sites, compared to our five million, smell is a dog's primary way of sensing and knowing about the world—including other dogs.

I know what you're thinking: "Their butts? Really? They connect by smelling each other's butts? That's where . . . "

And you're right. That's where the poop—and the stinky odor of poop—comes out. If you and I were sniffing a dog's butt, that's all we'd smell. I say that on faith, not experience. You can check it out for yourself if you want. But dogs have a second olfactory system in their noses, the Jacobson's organ, designed specifically for that all-important chemical communication. Nerves in that organ direct the meet-and-greet scents directly to the brain so they are not overpowered by parfum de poop. When a dog curls its lips and flares its nostrils, it opens up that organ to increase exposure of the nasal cavity to the aromatic delights of the other canine's posterior.

But buff sniffing wasn't enough for Daisy when Pippa and I stopped by. Daisy also wanted to hump her buddy, much to the embarrassment of her owner. As have millions of others, who've watched females and neutered males exhibiting this behavior, Bob and I joked about it too, theorizing Daisy probably had gender identity issues.

In truth, humping/mounting is fairly common canine behavior by neutered males, females, and even pups. "In fact, female dogs can be just as hump-happy as male dogs," said the *PetMD* website, which added the behavior is "normal," albeit often embarrassing for human owners and observers.

It certainly was embarrassing for me as a teen, as I was playing first base during a baseball game. A boxer ran out on the field, headed straight for me, and attempted to make mad, passionate doggy love to my leg. As I tried to shake him off and knock him away, people in the stands had a grand old time, laughing and directing mock "boos" my way for rejecting his advances.

Why do dogs do it? The American Kennel Club has some ideas:

- **They're excited.** Humping can be a sign of extreme excitement and is a common behavior seen in play, especially in places like dog parks.

- **They're stressed.** Dogs who feel nervous or anxious may mount other dogs or even objects near them, like a pillow.

- **They want attention.** If a dog is humping a person's leg, it's likely the person will reach down to push him away or (for small dogs) pick him up. By doing so, that person is rewarding the dog for the behavior. Even when received with what most owners would see as a clear refusal of attention (e.g., pushing away, scolding), the dog learns humping will get a response from his owner.

- **They want to gain social status.** Mounting can be a sign of dominance among dogs. Some dogs will even attempt to mount other dogs in a social setting to see which dogs will allow it and which won't. Unfortunately, this behavior can sometimes lead to fights and should be discouraged.

- **They find it pleasurable.** Mounting or humping can be a sexual behavior, even in dogs who have been spayed or neutered. Puppies may hump as "practice" for future sexual activities and intact dogs may use it as a form of flirting to entice mating.

- **They have a medical condition.** Certain medical conditions, such as urinary tract infections or even allergies, can cause your dog to hump more often than usual. Also, mental issues, such as a compulsive disorder or extreme anxiety, may be part of the problem.

I'm betting that boxer had mental issues. Possibly he escaped from an institution for canine sexual addicts. I definitely was not his type, and even if he had brought flowers and candy, I wasn't interested. With Daisy, I think it was excitement and most of the time Pippa didn't even notice.

* * * *

"Whenever Mrs. Kissel breaks wind, we beat the dog."
What discussion of dog butts would be complete without including farts? Whether human or canine, farts are funny, especially for those of us who've grown older but not up. I'll never forget the night I learned to light farts while I was in the Army. I didn't believe it was possible until I saw it with my own eyes. Then I laughed until my sides ached. And yes, some exceptional Americans can fart, as well as belch, at will. (Be certain to wear underwear if you try this.)

Go online, and you'll find lists for best fart scenes in movies. For my money, number one remains the beans-for-dinner-around-the-campfire sequence in Mel Brooks' movie *Blazing Saddles*. And I've always believed the title is a clever, but plausibly deniable, reference to that scene.

In the quotation above, Mrs. Kissel was the pastor's ancient housekeeper in Blake Edwards' movie *10*. After she set down a tea tray and was wobbling out of his study, she cut a long and loud one that sent a Great Dane scrambling out of the room. Thus, the quote.

Often, though, dogs *are* responsible. That's why someone has established a popular Facebook page touting April 8 as "Dog Farting Awareness Day." Thank goodness, Pippa thus far hasn't been a canine deserving of mention there. Despite her fondness for gobbling down disgusting morsels before I can stop her as we walk, I've yet to hear or smell a gaseous release. On the other hand, Ursa, her predecessor, could clear a room with her farts—and often did. Because they were silent, we had no time to escape before innocent noses were traumatized.

But as I said, farts are funny. No matter how awful the odor was, those of us engulfed by the noxious vapors laughed while fleeing. They can be humorous for other reasons as well. Bob said Daisy's were sometimes so loud she frightened herself.

And check out these comments I found online from the owners of potent pooches. Perhaps they weren't looking for laughs, but I'm betting you'll chuckle as you read them:

- "I have an English bulldog. He is TOXIC! He gets the proper diet, no human food, and his butt is always pointed toward me when he's lying down. As soon as I hear the familiar 'pphhttt,' I'm outta there. Car rides with him are torture."
- "I have a five-year-old rotten Rottie. He has gas so bad you can smell it before you see him."
- "We had a boxer for years and he was normal. We're on our second boxer now and Lord Almighty! I think I'm going to die soon of toxic poisoning."
- "I have a little Lhasa Apso. He doesn't fart much. But when he does, it routinely strips the paint off my ceiling. I mean it smells like a dead body pulled from a landfill. What's worse is that he seems to find it amusing. I'm on the floor vomiting and he's wagging his tail!. He's healthy, gets a good diet, walks, all of it. But his butt is toxic!"

If have a dog like one of those, *PetMD* suggests more exercise and smaller meals could help clear the air. Additionally, try providing the food in a quiet, non-competitive environment, if you aren't already. Make certain it is highly digestible. Sometimes changing food will help.

"Finally, be cautious about where your dog has access to food," *PetMD* said. "For example, put secure covers on garbage cans and do not let your dog roam into the neighbors' yards or into garages where garbage might be stored.

"Also, be observant about whether your dog is exhibiting coprophagia; that is, eating feces. For example, dogs especially will eat items like deer pellets because of their likeness to kibbles. If these changes do not help, schedule a visit with your veterinarian so an underlying disease may be ruled out as a cause for the excessive flatulence."

I don't know what Pippa thinks about deer pellets. But I'm convinced she believes rabbit droppings are Skittles.

18. One of a Kind

"Dogs come into our lives to teach us about love; they depart to teach us about loss. A new dog never replaces an old dog, it merely expands the heart. If you have loved many dogs, your heart is very big."

– Erica Jong

A horrible disease called degenerative myelopathy claimed my friend's dog this past spring. It began slowly, with her back legs occasionally collapsing in much the same way they would if she slipped on a wooden floor. Without warning, the process accelerated, and, within a few weeks she was nearly paraplegic. Just walking was arduous, and relieving herself without assistance was almost impossible.

Dealing with this was doubly difficult for Bob because Daisy, an 11-year-old black Lab, experienced no pain. In all other ways she was the same happy and affectionate dog she always had been since he adopted her from a shelter. She still wanted to run. She still wanted to play. She still wanted to walk down the hill in his backyard to do her business. But she couldn't.

And there's no recovering from degenerative myelopathy. It's irreversible, progressive, and a killer. From the back legs it moves to the front and then bodily functions, with complete paralysis the inevitable consequence.

Through research, my friend learned some people choose to build little two-wheel carts and other devices to enable their pets to get around. But such heroic measures do nothing to slow the disease. Rather, they simply allow the dogs to function for a few more months, with little or no quality of life.

Honestly, I wouldn't have been surprised if Bob chose that option. He'd been retired for a decade, and his entire life revolved around Daisy, along with caring for his yard and gardens. She followed him everywhere as he worked outside. He rarely left home because he didn't  want to leave her alone. She slept in his bed. Letting her outside was his reason to get up in the morning.

So when Bob called me and told me to bring Pippa over for one last visit with her best bud, Daisy, I was startled. But I also knew he was making the right choice, and I respected him for that. As we sat at his dining room table, watching the dogs greet, sniff, and generally pal around with each other for one last time, he told me, "I made Daisy a promise that when the time came I would do what's best for her."

I helped him take Daisy for her final visit to the veterinarian. We sat with her on the floor, stroked her head, and told her what a good girl she was, as the vet prepared the injection. "She knows," Bob said. "She knows."

I am not one to anthropomorphize animals, even dogs, who often seem so humanlike in communication skills with their owners. But I had to agree with Bob; I think that she did know. Those sad brown eyes, which had been so happy and lively when she was with Pippa just a few hours before, told us so.

As the weather warmed, Bob planted daisies down near the dock where the black Lab loved to go each evening to bark at the fish gathered there. He honored her with photos on the walls, including a collage I put together of pictures I'd taken over the years of Daisy, often playing with my Ursa, who had died four years before, and then with Pippa. I also included a quote from Will Rogers: "If there are no dogs in Heaven, then when I die, I want to go where they went."

Ursa, a red Lab/Rhodesian ridgeback mix, had been my companion for more than 13 years when I took her on that final trip to the vet, also in the spring. Then I waited nearly a year before adopting Pippa from the Farmington Pet Adoption Center. That was a mistake, a mistake I hoped that Bob would not make.

But nearly a year has passed, and he seems no closer now than he was the day after we said goodbye to Daisy. For a little while there, he did seem interested. I even drove more than 120 miles round trip with him to look at a dog at a shelter in St. Louis. And during that window when he seemed motivated, I visited the shelter where I adopted Pippa to see what was available. For some reason he wouldn't explore local options, and when I did find a dog that might be a good fit—a young adult female Lab mix—he refused to follow up.

I try not to be pushy when Pippa and I go to visit him now, but I know that sometimes, I am. Bob needs another canine companion; he needs a reason to get up in the morning. Right now, though, he's content to fawn over Pippa a couple of times a week, spoiling her with treats and affection when we visit.

"Daisy was one of a kind," he tells me. "I won't find another dog like her."

I know what he means. Daisy was special. She barked at every animal she saw on television, whether a horse, a lion, or the GEICO gecko. If it moved, she followed it across the screen and then looked for it outside the TV. Ursa and later Pippa, just cocked their heads with "what the heck is going on" expressions on their faces and watched her antics. Along with fish down at the dock, she also barked at floating leaves, a new lake sign on the nearby dam, and at voices she recognized on the telephone. Although she was a Lab, complete with webbed feet, she refused to go in the water. She liked to push her way between your legs so you'd scratch the base of her tail for her. When lying on the sofa, she often sighed in such a heartfelt and human-like way that you knew she loved life.

"You're right," I reply. "She was one of a kind.But every dog is one of a kind. That's what makes them so special. Ursa was one of a kind too. And so is Pippa.

"I waited too long to get Pippa too," I add. "I wish I hadn't."

I could tell Bob in much more detail about why Ursa was special and why Pippa is too, but don't. I've made my point and he won't get another dog until he thinks he'd ready. I hope it's soon. I have no doubt he will be happier for it.

Our conversation, meanwhile, does prompt me to recount my blessings in terms of my own special dogs, both of whom have been defined by their sweet, affectionate dispositions.

Without doubt, Ursa was the most laid back canine that I've ever met. I could run the vacuum cleaner over her—and often did—and she wouldn't budge. I taught her to catch a Frisbee, but early on she taught me that I had to throw it directly to her. She wasn't doing to chase it.

She didn't even acknowledge fireworks, thunder, or loud noises of any kind. She barked only when she heard someone approaching the front door. She liked to eat ice. She loved stuffed animals and, throughout her life, "adopted," but never destroyed, all she encountered. She once ate two batches of Christmas cookies from a metal tray on the kitchen counter without disturbing the cloth that had been covering them.

Contrary to Daisy, she didn't want to be touched by man nor beast anywhere near her tail. One of the few times I saw her show aggression toward another dog occurred when we met two golden retrievers and a husky on our morning walk. All were on leashes and all were friendly. But while the goldens and Ursa exchanged sniffs in the front, the husky explored forbidden territory. Ursa quickly rebuffed him with a ferocious snarl. As I was the alpha, she reluctantly allowed me to brush both sides of her tail when I groomed her, although she wasn't happy about it.

And the piece de resistance: If underwear and/or socks were left on the floor, especially by my girlfriend's daughter, Ursa ate them. We made this discovery in the "aftermath" of their consumption.

By contrast, Pippa is anything but laid back, her wariness perhaps at least in part a consequence of spending her first two years in a shelter. Thunder, fireworks, gunshots, and loud concussive noises of any sort send her scurrying to "anywhere but here," as if moving will put her out of range. She's also extremely sensitive to weather changes, and often becomes pensive long before low pressure and storms arrive.

On the other hand, she's also the happiest dog I've ever seen most of the time, but especially when the sun is out and we're alone. She displays it with her bouncing gait and the extravagant delight she derives from rolling on her back in grass and autumn leaves. She's the only dog I've ever seen who will chase a ball, catch it, and then toss it so she can chase it some more. She never barks.

Although shy, she never meets a stranger, either human, canine, or even feline. Her immediate instinct is to love them all, but her mad-dash approach can frightened the unwary, especially cats. Sometimes it takes more than one meeting before she will allow new friends to touch her. For the first few encounters she approaches as if eager to be petted, but then stops with head lowered and tail wagging madly, as she dances just out of range. And if more than two people are around, even if she knows them well, she's pensive and nervous, just as she would be if a storm were approaching. Possibly this behavior is a natural part of her. I tend to think it's more likely the canine equivalent of an anxiety disorder due to lack of socialization when she was a pup. Whatever the cause, it's a part of who Pippa is. I accept that, and even love her all the more because I know about her past and marvel at how far she has come as my companion. In return she accepts me with all my blemishes.

Only squirrels seem to be on her hit list, and, truly I think it's because they give her a reason to run. I don't know what she would do if she ever caught one, which doesn't seem likely. She has yet to learn that stealth often is more important than speed.

Her speed certainly can be frightening to some people, especially if they don't know her. In her enthusiasm to greet friends and strangers alike, she turns into a black streak of lightning. Thus, I put her on a leash when approaching people she doesn't know. And I yell "incoming" to friends who don't see or hear us approaching. The best part, though—and this is self-taught—is that Pippa never jumps on anyone, even the people she knows best. She speeds right up to them and sits down, her tail dancing, eager for them to acknowledge and pet her.

I could go on and onabout other ways that Pippa is special; about how she thinks water is alive, how she uses her nose as a tool to demand attention, and about how, for seemingly no reason other than to show her love for me, she'll walk under my hand and press against my leg as we are walking.

The routine developed by my friend Dave, his black Pekapoo, and his next-door neighbor provides one of my favorite examples of the intelligence and individuality of these amazing animals. The neighbor often babysits for BB, but Dave doesn't have to take his dog to her. Instead, he calls on the phone, and the Pekapoo, knowing what's coming, heads for the front door. My friend opens the door and BB streaks across his lawn, into the neighbor's driveway, and on into the house, where the neighbor is holding her door open. When it's time for BB to go home, the process is repeated in reverse. Her speedy flight from one house to another, ears flapping behind wildly in the breeze, is truly a treat to behold.

Yes, BB and Pippa are special, as were Ursa, Daisy, and millions of other dogs who bring joy every day to millions of owners. And many, many dogs confined in shelters could enrich so many lives if only people would adopt them.

Each dog is special because that is the essence of being a domesticated canine. Large or small, male or female, long hair or short, dogs exist to be loved and give love to humans and, in doing so, they reveal themselves to be just as unique in their individuality as are the people whose lives they enrich.

---

19. Christmas

I couldn't stay in bed any longer. The digital clock revealed the time was only 6:30, a half hour before I usually get up. Dim light filtering through the blinds suggested yet another day would dawn dull and gray. The weather was cold too. I had every reason to hunker down under my grandmother's quilt and the down comforter for at least another half hour—or until Pippa, accustomed to our schedule, came in to tell me she was ready for our morning walk.

Yes, it was Christmas morning, not a time for sleeping in, as any kid will tell you. I fondly remembered all those mornings when I was a child. And, as I often have as an adult, I felt far more appreciation for what my parents did to make me happy than I ever did back then. I wish they were alive for me to tell them.

But they are not, and I'm not a kid. Santa didn't come. There were no presents under the little decorated tree sitting on my dining room table. And although I hung stockings for Pippa and me on the mantle, I hadn't put anything in them. What was the hurry? Sad to say, this was just another early winter's morning for an aging bachelor and his dog.

As I lay there in the near dark, perhaps what pushed me out of bed early was memories of wonderful Christmases past when Santa Claus was real, the holiday was magic, and I tossed and turned most all of the never-ending night. These memories conflicted my mind because they "hurt so good." Perhaps it was mental regression, an inevitable consequence of growing old—a likelihood I didn't want to confront. Maybe I always did this on Christmas morning but just didn't remember. Yikes.

Deciding it was better not to dwell on such things, I hastened to dress. Pippa whined eagerly as I pulled on my hiking boots. I wished her "Merry Christmas" as I gently squeezed the fur on her neck and looked into those bright, brown eyes. She's just a dog, though, so she didn't know what I was talking about. But, deferential and polite as always, she wagged her tail anyway. And we were off.

Outside, the early morning was drenched in cold pewter, as I expected. Following a little rain the night before and with no wind to push it away, mist lingered in the heavy air. No white Christmas. No bright Christmas. Rather a day that would make anyone with seasonal affective disorder inconsolable and desiring copious quantities of adults-only egg nog. Although such weather typically doesn't trouble Pippa as much as wind, rain, and thunder, neither is it her favorite. She tends to be subdued in such conditions, preferring to walk with me and saving bouncy jubilance for mornings with blue skies and an eager sun on the horizon.

Yet, on this silent, gray day, she was as happy and excited as I'd ever seen her—much like a child at Christmas. She pranced down the road in front of me, streaked back to urge me on, and then bolted forward again. At a fenced backyard she paused to wish season's greetings to a black and white cat sitting on a stump. As she always does when happy, she lowered her head and bounced a time or two, as if extending it an invitation to play. Although I'm not fluent in feline, I believe the cat's response was something on the order of "Bah! Humbug!"

But that didn't deter Pippa's celebratory manner and gait. Nor did the absence of her friends, the mallard ducks, at the lake, still covered with ice from a recent freeze. Because she doesn't bark and runs with the silence of a shadow, she often gets within a few feet of the ducks before they grumpily take note. They paddle away, quacking something that I suspect is not, "Good morning."

With no fowl to see and nothing foul to hear, Pippa paused briefly to survey the barren lake. Then she darted on toward the civilized portion of our unique rural-suburban community, featuring a paved road and traffic. And as I called her to me so I could snap on her leash, I smiled at what we soon would see—penguins and a polar bear, animals from opposite ends of the planet, coming together in someone's yard to celebrate the holiday season. The inflatables intrigued Pippa each time we passed, and she would have inspected them more closely if not on a leash. This morning, though, they were flat and lifeless. No smiling penguins perched on presents. No happy polar bear hefting a snow ball.

A crabby cat. No ducks, no penguins, no polar bears. Poor Pippa. But her joy would not be denied. Once I turned her loose in a wooded area again, she burst forth to greet her good buddies, the squirrels. On a dull, gray day in which such emotions seemed wildly inappropriate, she still could not contain her happiness and enthusiasm as, one after another, she hastened their mad scramble up oak trees.

It was almost as if . . . Well, that wasn't possible. She's just a dog. But it was almost as if Pippa knew it was Christmas and was celebrating, not just the holiday and the birth of Jesus Christ, but the life-altering gift we both received when I stopped by the Farmington Pet Adoption Center nearly four years earlier.

She's just a dog, though. She couldn't know. She couldn't know she had two strikes against her back then and that the odds of being adopted were slim and none. She couldn't know being black was strike one because such dogs are considered bad luck and tend to be overlooked among lighter colored canines. She couldn't know that being an adult was strike two. People want puppies and adult dogs usually aren't even a consideration.

No, she's just a dog. She didn't remember she spent the first two years of her life in confinement. She didn't recognize that she was born to run, and she couldn't appreciate that now she could do so with abandon every day of the week.

She couldn't know she survived heartworm infection while at the kennel, as well as two bouts with the mange.

No, she's just a dog. She couldn't appreciate that she received toys and treats as Christmas presents from neighbors and friends.

She couldn't value the luxury of three soft beds, one in her kennel, another under the stairs, and a third in front of a French door, perfect for soaking up the afternoon sun.

She couldn't know how fortunate we were to be re-united after she was frightened by firecrackers that first summer and ran away in blind panic. Perhaps it was a Christmas miracle in July that she was taken in two days later and ten miles away by a kind family, who found me through Facebook.

No, she's just a dog.

* * * * *

Pippa couldn't know that her visits now are a highlight for my friend, Bob, who lives alone and still refuses to get another dog following the death of his beloved Daisy. Also, on more than one occasion, he told me that Christmas is his least favorite time.

On Christmas Eve, he eagerly greeted her at the door. As always, I had to squeeze around Bob and Pippa just to get inside. He talked to her nearly as much as he talked to me, smothered her with affection, and spoiled her with treats. When it was time to leave, he went outside with us—possibly his first trip out of doors that day—and we watched as Pippa performed her usual routine in his yard. She ran manic laps around us, jumped drainage ditches, and rolled in piles of dead leaves. She teased us the same way she would tease Scrooge the cat the next morning, but, unlike the feline, Bob was delighted. He teased her right back, prompting more warp speed orbits around us.

As we laughed I told Bob, probably for the 1,000th time, "She does this all the time. She makes me happy every day." I left unspoken what I really wanted to say, "Bob, it's time for you to get another dog."

Before we left, he volunteered to babysit for Pippa on Christmas Day while I had dinner at my niece's house. Pippa doesn't need a babysitter. In fact, she seems to enjoy some "me" time, possibly because of living constantly among her much more vocal brethren at the shelter for two years. I thanked him but was noncommittal.

On Christmas Day, though, I decided it wasn't about Pippa needing or not needing a babysitter. After we returned from our morning walk, I called Bob and took him up on his offer. Maybe I did so because of the gift Pippa just had given me. Maybe not. I don't know. It just seemed the right thing to do.

When I dropped her off, she ran directly to the crock, where my friend keeps the dog treats, and didn't even see me leave. I had visions of returning hours later to find my once, slender companion with a double chin and bulging belly.

Yes, she probably ate more treats in those few hours than I give her in a week. But that's okay. As I pulled back in the driveway that evening, I saw the two of them sitting by the crock, with Bob gently stroking her head.

Inside, Pippa bounded to meet me and I thanked Bob for babysitting. "Better than being alone on Christmas Day," he said.

He also told me she'd been frightened by a noise, so he coaxed her up on the sofa with him, where they stayed for an hour or so. Staying in any place for an hour was unusual for Pippa, to say the least.

Of course, I'm not suggesting she understood Bob's loneliness, and stayed there because of that. She doesn't know how much he needs another canine companion. She's just a dog.

But I know. I also know that her joyous demeanor earlier that day on a dull, dreary Christmas morning, as a present for me, ranked right up there with the bicycle and electric train Santa brought long, long ago.

Back at home, I gave her treats—as if she needed them following four-plus hours at Bob's house—and, as I had earlier that day, said, "Merry Christmas" as I pulled her close for a hug.

With our faces near, Pippa looked me in the eyes, and I swear I saw something in hers. It might have been, "Merry Christmas."

More likely it was "Got any more chicken jerky?"

After all, she's just a dog.

20. Superstitious Minds

"**B**lack dogs are tough to find homes for," the shelter staffer revealed to me, just as I was ready to take Pippa home. "They're like black cats. People don't want them."

I was stunned by her words. I might have decided not to take Pippa if she barked too much, was uncontrollable on a leash, too aggressive, or possibly threatening toward strangers. But rejecting her because of her black coat, complemented by a little white on her chest and toes, never occurred to me.

Then again, if I decided to adopt a cat, color wouldn't have been a major consideration either. Perhaps I'm different from the norm. Now that I think of it, of course I am. I'm the "weird uncle." Or to put it another way, the black sheep of my family. And there's that word again. Sheep aren't spared either. That superstition supposedly came from Scotland, where farmers believed the birth of a black sheep spelled doom for the remainder of the flock. Also, the fleece of a black sheep was less valuable because of the difficulty in dyeing it.

But black dogs?

When I checked with other shelters and workers in veterinarians' offices, they told me much the same thing. I even found a website devoted to the subject, *Blackpearldogs.com*, with heartbreaking comments from shelters. Here's an example:

"We are guessing that the general public is not aware of how doomed black dogs are when they are brought to a pound because black dogs, particularly black Labs or Lab mixes, are euthanized at a horrifying rate at many pounds and shelters because people pass them up for lighter colored dogs."

On the flip side, I was heartened to find a book celebrating the beauty of black dogs, *Black is Beautiful, a Celebration of Dark Dogs*, by Pamela Black Townsend. Published in 2007, it's now out of print and copies seem generally unavailable. Sadly, maybe there's a connection between the unpopularity of black dogs and books written about them.

Winston Churchill figures prominently in one of my most startling discoveries. "Black dog" long has been a metaphor for depression, and the British leader who so inspired his people with reassuring speeches during World War II referred to his lifelong struggle as his "black dog." Some historians believe the term began with English nannies who explained their early morning surliness by saying, "I have got a black dog on my back today."

As I researched black dogs, I expanded my search into dog superstitions in general and found some interesting, humorous, and downright bizarre beliefs. But before I share some of those, I want to say this about black dogs:

"Black dog" might be a synonym for depression. Black dogs, along with black cats, might be considered bad luck. Black dogs may be overlooked in shelters in favor of those with lighter colored coats.

But Pippa, my black dog who endured the first two years of her life in a shelter, is the quintessential antidote for depression. Every morning she makes me happy. As she whines, paces, and bounces, eager to begin our walk, she also demands to be petted. She darts in with her long nose, knocking my hands away from my shoes as I try to tie them. Out the door, she prances down the drive and up the gravel road. If I'm not fast enough, she scurries back, as if to say, "Get the lead out."

She trees squirrels and wonders where they went, looking about with an almost comical expression. She feints a charge at ducks along the shoreline of a lake, just to hear them fuss and squawk. And always, always, she rolls on her back, whether in snow, leaves, or grass, moaning in delight as her tongue wags and her brown eyes roll, as if she's never experienced anything so delightfully decadent until that very moment. All of that and more that she does daily make me smile and laugh. Maybe Pippa acts this way because she's a natural comedian. Or maybe she is especially appreciative of life because of her time in a shelter. All I know is, it isn't possible to be depressed around my black dog. She won't allow it.

Of course, she would be this way no matter the color of her coat. But it isn't another color. It's black. And as Pippa has shown me, black dogs are beautiful, both inside and out.

*   *   *   *

Looking for information about the bad reputation endured by black dogs led me to some amusing discoveries. This probably is my favorite:

If you step in dog poop with your left foot, you'll receive good luck. But if you do so with your right, bad luck will come. Who but the French could give us such a superstition? Possibly, it originated as a joke, for the streets of Paris are sometimes a minefield of dog poop, even though it's been illegal for owners to leave the wastes behind since 1982. Unlike most dog-owning citizens of cities in the

U.S., Parisians don't feel obligated to clean up after their pooches. Having been to the City of Light, I have first-hand knowledge of that. I have many fond memories of my time there, but washing dog poop off the bottom of my shoe in a bidet is not one of them.

On a website entitled *Rue Rude*, I found this delightful tidbit:

"Paris lovers try not to notice the dog poop everywhere, but they have to be careful anyway. In my neighborhood, if you don't have your eyes riveted on the sidewalk as you walk, you will have a nasty surprise on your shoes when you get home. Hundreds of people a year wind up in the hospital after slipping in dog poop. One of them was our ancient concierge, who died from the fall."

In 2013, Eleanor Beardsley, an NPR correspondent living in Paris, offered this:

"When you walk down the grand boulevards of the City of Light, you have to be careful where you step. Every day, my senses are assaulted by the piles I have to dodge in the Parisian streets. There are the fresh ones that leave me feeling angry, and the ones from the previous days that have begun to smear down the street on the bottoms of people's shoes."

Based on vast personal experience, I'd have to say that stepping in dog poop is more bad than good, no matter which foot is involved—especially if you're going barefoot or wearing sandals. Although I haven't kept records, I'm sure my left foot has "stepped in it" as often as my right, and I don't remember any good luck that followed. Ursa, predecessor to Pippa and her polar opposite in energy, was instrumental in my education about this. She preferred to relieve herself as close to doors as possible.

In Scotland, meanwhile, many people believe that if a dog follows you home, you will be granted good luck, and even more so if the dog is black. How about that? Additionally, if the dog enters your house, a new and valued friendship likely will follow.

Ursa, Pippa, and I have had four dogs follow us home and I've reunited all of them with their owners. I don't remember any specific good luck that followed for me, although Pippa and Ursa might have experienced otherwise and just didn't tell me. What I can tell you, though, is that seeing the happiness on the faces of those people who got their beloved pets back was gratifying beyond measure.

Here are a few more weird, wacky, and downright mystifying superstitions related to dogs:

- When a dog is staring intently, at nothing, for no apparent reason, look between the dog's ears and you'll see a ghost.
- A dog walking between a courting couple indicates a quarrel will soon take place or the wedding may be cancelled.
- In India, some people believe a woman will be impregnated with puppies if she is bitten by a dog.
- Three white dogs seen together mean good luck.
- If your dog doesn't like someone, it's because that person is dishonest or of bad character. (Most of us probably believe that one, right?)
- A home where a well-cared for, happy greyhound lives never will be haunted by malicious spirits.
- If a black dog appears in your car when you're driving alone, you are in danger of an accident. (I'd say that if *any* dog appears in my car while I'm driving, I'm in danger of an accident. Same for a cat, bird, or my dear, departed grandparents.)
- Seeing an ambulance is unlucky unless you pinch your nose or hold your breath until you see a black or brown dog. (Only problem with that is if you follow this advice, you probably will need the ambulance.)
- If your newborn baby is licked by a dog, it will be a quick healer. (Just don't tell the baby where else that tongue has been.)

- If a dog lies on its back, it's going to rain. A dog eating grass signifies the same thing, as does a canine sitting with cross forepaws. And, just like when you wash your car, if you give your dog a bath, rain will follow. (But even if you never wash your car or your dog, it's still going to rain—eventually.)
- And, finally, a practice I always follow when I want to keep a dog I've just adopted: Measure its tail with a cornstalk and bury the cornstalk under the front step.

21. The Secret Life of Pets

One morning, I noticed the top of Pippa's left hindquarter, near her tail, was wet. Not just damp, but soaked. Of course, I asked her about it. She declined comment, preferring instead to indicate by whining and pacing that I should hasten to put on my shoes and open the door so she could defend our homestead from squirrels.

The next morning, the same place on her body was soaked. And the next. And the next. She obviously was chewing and/or licking herself repeatedly during the night. Sometimes the target area would be larger than others, but always the same focal point.

Fearful now that she might have a raw "hot spot" under her black hair, I searched and found nothing. The skin seemed fine, even as the routine continued. She never showed the slightest inclination during the day to do whatever she was doing to herself at night, when I was asleep and she was in the basement. She has two "dens" down there, and they are where she prefers to spend the night, as opposed to upstairs with me.

For lack of a better word, I'd call Pippa an "independent" dog when she's in the house with me. My theory is that she never had any "me" time during her first two years, when she was one among many at a no-kill shelter. So now she's enjoys occasionally being by herself. And not only at night. Although she has the run of the house, she spends considerable time alone in the basement, even after four years as my companion.

By contrast, when we're outside, riding in the car, and visiting friends, she's my shadow, except when she breaks away briefly to tree a squirrel. But then she comes right back to me. During the past few months she's been spending more and more time with me upstairs during the day, indicating she's still adapting to a life of freedom. Typically, she comes up the stairs, pads over to my recliner-office, and bangs the bottom of my elbow with her long nose, demanding affection.

Incredibly, she just did that very thing while I wrote this. As I stroked her head and gently squeezed both sides of her neck, she sat to enjoy the affection. When I stopped too soon, she nudged me again with her nose. I petted her some more, and, as she sometimes does, she lifted one of her paws and placed it over my arm. She then walked over to a bed I keep near a French door so she can nap in the afternoon sun.

By the way, studies suggest that male dogs, and cats too, use their left paws more, and females their right. But Pippa seems to be ambidextrous.

Only her left hindquarter, however, was being abused each night. When she was out of my sight, what in the world was going on?

Thinking that one of her basement beds might be the source an allergic reaction, I washed them both. No luck. She continued to lick/chew each night until, one morning, I did notice a small raw spot.

The vet confirmed my diagnosis and provided three medications, one a topical spray to relieve itch, another an anti-inflammatory, and the third an antibiotic. I used them all as directed—or at least I attempted to.

The first time I found one of the little white pills on the floor, I assumed I'd been careless in giving it to Pippa the previous evening. I scolded myself for not being more thorough.

So, that night I pried open Pippa's jaws, dropped in the pill, held her mouth closed, and stroked her neck. She swallowed. Job done. Anti-inflammatory now doing its job.

And the next morning I found the little white pill on her bed. Huh? How was that possible? I had a mystery on my hands, no doubt about it.

The third time I tried, I opened Pippa's jaws after she swallowed and peered inside. And, sure enough, there was the little white pill tucked in behind her gum at the base of her upper jaw. How did she do that? How could she maneuver her tongue in such a way to move such a tiny object up there while I held her jaws closed?

She wouldn't tell me, so I still don't know. Eventually I administered all of the medications, as the vet prescribed. But to no avail. Pippa kept licking/chewing. So now it was time for a little Yankee ingenuity. I put a pair of my jockey shorts on her, and secured them with a bungee cord. They were green, by the way. I cut a slit in the bottom so her tail could stick through.

Besides humans, only the dog can so exquisitely convey humiliation with a look, and Pippa was no exception. But the jockey shorts worked, and from time to time, I continue to employ them. And I still don't have a clue why she's so fixated on her left hindquarter.

Nor do I know why she's always upstairs when I return home, even though she seems to be most comfortable in the basement. Of course, I don't get to see what she's doing up there. As I open the door into the basement from the tuck-under garage, she comes running down the stairs to greet me. I don't think she's using the computer, since I always check the browsing history and have found nothing suspicious. The television isn't warm either, and it's always tuned to the same channel as when I turned it off. I did notice once that my bag of Zapp's Voodoo Chips seemed a little emptier than I remembered. But a breathalyzer test showed nothing.

Pippa doesn't shed much, except for a couple of times a year. That means it's difficult to find evidence if she's getting on the sofa or, like Goldilocks, sleeping in my bed.

In other words, I have nothing to complain about in terms of what she's doing when I am not home, especially when I hear stories of the messes and destruction wrought by other people's dogs when left alone. They shred curtains and furniture. They chew pillows and shoes. They turn over trash cans, eat, and spread garbage, including—shudder—used feminine hygiene products, all over the place.

Or when I watch some of the videos posted on the internet, filmed by dog owners when they were out of the house, especially the one that features a wiry haired little dog dragging his butt back and forth across the sofa. Yikes!

I was fortunate with Pippa's predecessor Ursa, as well. Her only transgressions that I know of included gobbling up Christmas cookies as they cooled on the kitchen counter and consuming underwear and socks left on the floor by my girl friend's daughter.

My sister, meanwhile, had a dachshund named Max who ate an entire package of Hershey's kisses. And, yes, his poop was, shall we say, rather metallic for awhile. Fortunately, all that foil didn't block his intestines and the candy was milk chocolate instead of dark. The darker and more bitter the chocolate, the more of a health threat it poses to dogs because of the methylxanthines (caffeine and theobromine) it contains. In sufficient amounts, they can cause muscle tremors, seizures, internal bleeding, and even heart attacks in our canine friends.

When dogs eat cookies, candy, and other usually forbidden food, the fault generally lies with people who failed to put the food out of reach. After all, canines are led by their noses, which are far more sensitive than ours. And if they smell food of any kind and no one is around to tell them not to . . .

Other types of misbehavior, meanwhile, can often be explained by too much pent up energy, boredom, or anxiety. Contrary to what some believe, dogs are not motivated by the desire to "get even" for being left alone.

"The truth is, dogs don't misbehave out of spite. They just aren't capable of that emotion. Humans are the only animals that can understand and act out of revenge. While dogs *do* feel emotions, most experts agree they aren't wired to plan ahead. They live completely in the moment," explains Pedigree Dog Food on its website.

"That's why the *only* time to correct a dog for naughty behavior is when you catch him in the act. Dragging your dog back to the scene of the crime doesn't help because he doesn't remember committing the crime. So, yelling at the dog when you find poop on the rug only communicates that you're angry, not what you're angry about. Your dog doesn't associate the feces—or the fact that he defecated on the rug—with your anger.

"If you've accused your dog of 'spiteful' behavior because he misbehaves when you're gone, it's time to rethink the situation. Your dog isn't trying to get back at you for leaving him alone. His bad behavior is probably just the result of his anxiety and stress about being alone, or his boredom."

One simple solution for curtailing the misbehavior could be simply spending more time playing with and walking your dog. It's good for both of you. Dog Whisperer Cesar Milan recommends taking him for a long walk to burn off energy before you leave the house. Also put all items your pet isn't allowed to chew or bite out of reach, while providing chew toys to keep him occupied.

"To encourage appropriate chewing in a destructive dog, engage him in play with chew toys on a daily basis and give him lots of fuss when he shows in interest in toys," says *The Daily Puppy* website."This teaches him that chewing the appropriate toys has a positive outcome."

And right in keeping with this theory that dogs understand only anger and not its cause, I offer the embarrassing evidence that sometimes, when Pippa is near, I yell at the computer for its blatant disregard in typing what I intended, or the television because someone on the screen is distorting the truth—at least my version of the truth. And my poor puppy starts to scurry away, thinking I must be mad at her. For Pippa and other dogs, life is all about what's happening in the moment. And if she and I are the only ones in the room, and I'm yelling . . . it must be at her. I am trying to do better.

Which brings us to cats, which, in my opinion, never try to do better. Rather, they delight in bringing chaos and destruction to the world when left home alone. A dog pees on the carpet while you're gone, right out there where you will notice upon your return. A cat goes in the closet and pees in one of your shoes. A dog chews on the highly visible leg of a table. A cat shreds the rarely seen back of the sofa.

And when cats and dogs are left home alone together, the felines are like the kids in school who come up with ideas for the stunts and pranks that get their classmates in trouble, as they sit back and watch the fun.

"Go ahead, chew on that shoe. It's an old one. He won't mind.

"Go ahead. It's a trash can. He won't mind if you eat what's inside.

"Go ahead. Dig around in that litter and you'll find some treats!"

Just so you know, though, I do like cats. They are clever, inquisitive animals and a delight to watch at play, especially when young. Also, they're typically lower maintenance than dogs, with the aforementioned litter box being a notable exception and a deal breaker for me. But while dogs are loyal by disposition, cats are independent. In other words, I don't trust 'em! In the wild, I'd much rather come face to face with a pack of wolves than a mountain lion.

My aversion to cats, I am embarrassed to confess, likely stems from an incident that perhaps scarred me when I was a teen. Peppy, our seal point Siamese cat, was sleeping in my lap one lazy Saturday afternoon as I relaxed in my father's recliner and watched college football. Suddenly, she shattered the quiet with an ear-piercing shriek, jumped up, dug the claws of all four paws through my jeans and into my legs, and then bolted from the room. Should I ever hear anyone say cats don't have nightmares, I will drop my pants and show them evidence that suggests otherwise.

By contrast, I've never seen a dog behave this way. Rather, as they dream, they lie peacefully on their sides, paws moving reflexively, as they whistle softly through their noses, chasing squirrels and rabbits.

And maybe cats. I hope it's cats. Come to think of it, maybe that was Peppy's nightmare.

22. Adopting an Adult Dog

"If you don't own a dog, at least one, there is not necessarily anything wrong with you, but there may be something wrong with your life."

— *Roger Caras*

We don't adopt adult humans. Why would we want to adopt adult dogs?

Puppies are cute, cuddly, and playful. For that reason and several others, most people don't consider an adult dog when they decide to adopt a canine companion. I used to feel the same way. One of my fondest memories of Ursa occurred on the day I brought her home. As I shaved in front of the bathroom mirror, I was startled to see her reflection as she playfully ran behind me, unfurling the

toilet tissue from its holder. Because they have no history, puppies are generally easy to train. Ursa learned commands quickly, and by using crate confinement for a few days, was easy to housebreak.

I know that I certainly didn't expect to adopt an adult dog when I went to the Farmington Pet Adoption Center that February day. I wanted a pup.

But none were available. I almost left, with the intention of waiting a bit in hopes a pup would come in—or I could look elsewhere. Still, I'd driven 25 miles, so I decided I might as well check out the adult dogs.

Four years later, I couldn't be happier that I chose Pippa, a two-year-old mixed breed who spent her first two years of life at the shelter. Yes, it's been an adventure for both of us, as she learned about the outside world and I learned that dealing with an adult dog instead of a pup isn't necessarily more difficult. It's just different.

Since then, I've made it a mission to encourage others to adopt adult dogs. Along the way, I learned about the tragic circumstances that often put dogs in shelters. Yes, many are intentionally dumped along roads by unconscionable people. Others get lost or separated from their owners. Some are turned over to shelters because their masters can no longer care for them. And sometimes their owners die.

These dogs need homes, but sadly, many of them never get a second chance. They are killed because few people want to adopt them and shelters simply can't care for them all. The American Society for the Prevention of Cruelty to Animals estimates about 3.9 million dogs go to shelters each year and 1.2 million are euthanized. Other sources say those numbers are much higher, as many go unreported.

"Shelter staffers often shake their heads as families pass up ideal, kid-friendly adult dogs in favor of pups of some highly inappropriate breed or type, just because they are puppies," dog trainer Pat Miller said in *The Whole Dog Journal*.

"There are a multitude of benefits when you bring an adult dog into your family. You don't have to deal with those nasty-sharp puppy teeth. And because your dog has her adult teeth, she's less likely to chew everything within her reach."

That certainly has been the case with Pippa. Since the first day, she hasn't chewed on anything except bones and an occasional stick she picks up when feeling especially playful outside.

Miller explained that an adult dog, if not housetrained, at least has the physical ability to hold bowels and bladder for longer periods of time, "and can usually learn appropriate bathroom habits quickly, with proper management and training."

She also said an adult dog can be a ready-made exercise buddy because it is capable of more physical activity than a puppy. Pippa fit the bill there as well. We walk twice a day, every day.

"As an added benefit, you have that feel-good feeling that comes with adopting a dog who might otherwise not find a forever home," Miller added.

But do practice due diligence before you decide to adopt. Ask questions about the dog's background and health history. Depending on how it was acquired, shelter staffers may be able to tell you everything—or nothing. Also, take it for a "test walk" as I did with Pippa. Observe its behavior, both in confinement and among people and other dogs. Heed your instincts.

Also, keep in mind that whatever circumstances put a dog in a shelter, especially an adult dog that bonded with its original owner, it will be stressed for awhile, and possibly even feel extreme anxiety.

"Dogs that permanently lose their masters, their 'family,' are subject to particularly serious emotion trauma, and the symptoms of this are exactly the same as those of children suffering the same fate," said Vilmos Csanyi, a dog behavior expert at Eotvos Lorand University in Budapest, Hungary.

"A dog that has become a burden and is tossed out of a car and left to its own fate will search for its master for days, will not eat, and suffers visibly.

"Anyone who rids himself of his erstwhile pet in such a fashion may delude himself by thinking that it is only an animal," he continued. "Such a person does not realize that dogs are as capable of suffering as humans and are the exception among animals in that they experience rejection similarly to humans and human children."

Worried about whether an adult dog can bond with you as a puppy would? Csanyi insists you shouldn't worry. "Dogs are able even in old age to develop lasting and deep attachments if their love and bonding are reciprocated," he said.

Possibly because he's seen what a loving companion that Pippa is for me, my friend Bob finally decided to adopt an adult dog following the death of his black Lab, Daisy. Searching online, he found a Lab mix he liked at a shelter about 65 miles away. But when we arrived, we learned she was on medication for anxiety, and the shelter workers knew nothing of her history. We drove home without the dog.

Because of what I've learned and my experience with Pippa, I probably would have adopted the dog had I been in search of a new companion. No adult dog comes ready-to-go, with no effort required, and that certainly was the case with Pippa.

She didn't suffer the separation anxiety that sometimes occurs with adult dogs, probably because she grew up in a shelter and had bonded with no one. But she was skittish, especially in regard to new people and sudden movements. Brisk winds made her nervous. Short rides in the car made her sick. And certain loud noises—thunder, fireworks, cars backfiring—sent her into mindless panic.

Pippa still is a bit nervous today and likely to pace if a storm is approaching. But I've taken her for walks on a leash with the sound of thunder still far away to help her settle down, and she has. I've taken her for progressively longer and longer drives, and now she loves to ride in the car. Also she has bonded with me, which went a long way toward making her feel safe and secure.

Here is what Pippa taught me about adopting an adult dog:

1. It takes time

I adopted Pippa in late February, but she didn't fully bond with me until July. When I returned from a weekend business trip in early May and picked her up at the kennel, she didn't even respond. It was as if she's never seen me before. But when I let her out of the car back at home, she clearly was happy; she recognized that as the place that she wanted to be.

By mid-summer, though, we were connected. If frightened, instead of trying to run away, she came immediately to my side and leaned against my leg. Today, she's affectionate and often walks up to and under my hand so I will pet her.

Still, she spent much of her life alone in a kennel, and that influences her behavior. At night she chooses to go to the basement and sleep there by herself. Only recently, has she started to spend as much time upstairs with me as downstairs by herself. If we're experiencing unsettled weather, she will retreat to the bathroom or the basement.

Overall, she is a dog so bursting with happiness that it is infectious.

2. Housebreaking

The bad news is I've been unable to housebreak Pippa. The good news is that she's peed and pooped in the house only a couple of times, and both of those occurred within weeks of adoption.

She was so accustomed to going to the bathroom in her kennel whenever she wanted to that I've been unable to get her to associate going outside with relieving herself. She simply doesn't understand. I've even tried teaching by example, but to no avail.

Probably I could get her to make the connection by using confinement in a crate when she's inside. But I chose not to do that.

On the positive side, she waits to poop and pee until we go on morning and evening walks. Keeping to a consistent schedule, I think, is the key. Also, for several months, I picked up her water bowl each night to prevent those long, late-night drinks that might prompt an "accident."

3. The outside world

Dogs who spend much of their lives in confinement know little about the outside world. They often are more easily frightened by loud noises and/or sudden movements than are puppies. Pippa is certainly that way, especially in regard to thunder and fireworks. As a result, I take extra precautions around the Fourth of July to be sure she stays safe.

Also, many of these dogs don't bark, and that's the case for Pippa. But I know she can bark because she did it twice when frightened. Otherwise, she is silent except for whining, which is what she often does as she waits for my neighbor to open his patio door so she can go inside for treats.

And everything is new. In the beginning Pippa chased falling leaves, snowflakes, and anything else that moved. Also, she continues to see moving water as something alive. She loves to wade into the lake to cool off and splash about. But as she does, she makes waves that frighten her out. Over time, it turned into a game.

In general, life with Pippa is a game now that we've adjusted to one another. She makes me smile every day as she rolls joyously in the grass, bounces with eagerness before every walk, and runs laps around me to burn off excess energy when we haven't hiked far enough to satisfy her.

In short, choosing Pippa was one of the best decisions I ever made, and it likely wouldn't have happened if a pup had been available. When the time comes for you to get a new companion, I hope you'll remember my experience and consider an adult dog. Millions of them are looking for homes.

23. Adopting an Adult Human
By Pippa

"I've seen a look in dogs' eyes, a quickly vanishing look of amazed contempt, and I am convinced that basically dogs think humans are nuts."

—*John Steinbeck*

Thinking of going home with a human? If so, you need to know some things. I can help you there.

First you should know that I'm called Pippa. Who knows where my human got that name, but I'm okay with it. It kinda fits, you know? It feels right. Back in the day when I was doing time, I was called "Barb," which I didn't like much. But, hey, I got two squares a day and a place to sleep, so I wasn't complaining.

I can't remember what life was like before the shelter because I was too young. I just remember growing up there, sharing the yard with all those other dogs, and no privacy. I didn't like that. But the people at the shelter were kind and they took care of me when I was sick.

Most of the humans who came in looking for a new companion were kind too. Being a dog yourself, you know we can tell things like that right away. It's the smell and the vibe. Right?

Rule No. 1: Don't go home with just anyone.

Some aren't a good fit. For me, that included those little humans who came in with the big ones. They were cute, like puppies with two legs. But they were too noisy for me, and living in the shelter I had my fill of that already. Some of those dogs never shut up. And when humans came in, there was all kinds of acting out to get their attention. I never understood that.

Me? I wanted someone who gave off "quiet" vibes, if you know what I mean. Maybe, though, you'd like to be around little humans. I'm not one to judge.

Big humans with fur all over their faces scared me too. Why? Who knows? Why are some humans afraid of mice or spiders?

So, if the smell and the vibe weren't right, I'd just hang back while the rest of dogs made fools of themselves. Being black, I wasn't easily noticed, unless visitors took their time. Mostly they were distracted by my noisy cellmates, which was fine with me.

Then this one big human came in with no little ones and no fur on his face. Also, he took his time and read the information on each of the cells about the dogs in them. I don't think he liked all that noise either.

I decided to come forward and get a closer look at him. The smell and the vibe were good. He smiled. Okay, I thought, this might be the one. But I needed a closer look, so I reared up on the wire to show him I was interested.

He left and then a shelter human came back with a leash. I had seen this drill before and the other dogs told me what happened. All right! I was going to get a closer smell of him outside.

We went for a walk. It was good. Away from all those other dogs, his scent was even better. It smelled like home. I know that sounds strange, but it was true. He was the one for me. I hoped he thought so too.

And he did! A few days later he came to take me to my new home. I was nervous, but generally happy about that. But when he put me in the backseat of his car, I got scared, especially in my stomach. I had never ridden a car.

Rule No. 2: When you're going to your new home, try to relax. It's not easy, I know. You're happy, excited, scared and all kinds of other things. But if you pace, it just makes things worse. Chill out. Lie down. Or sit and look out the window. Otherwise, your new human will have a mess to clean up in the backseat when you get home, and that's not a good way to start a relationship. I was glad he took the precaution of covering his back seat with a sheet.

Rule No. 3: At your new home, eat just a little at first, to give your tummy time to adjust to new food. Otherwise, your new human will be cleaning up yet another mess.

Rule No. 4: Don't relieve yourself or mark territory in the house. Humans don't like that. Yeah, I know. What's that about? Anyway . . . Chances are you won't be able to resist doing that once or twice, as they develop a schedule for taking you out. Be patient with them.

Rule No. 5: Don't give in to temptation. Being in a shelter, you haven't gnawed on anything in awhile. Believe me, I understand. And at your new home you'll see all kinds of things that look chewable, including furniture legs and shoes. Don't do it! If your human is as smart as mine, he or she will have bones and toys for you, and will put other stuff out of reach.

Rule No. 6: Stay off the furniture, unless you're invited on. Humans don't like presumptuous dogs. And they should provide you with a nice comfortable bed, much better than what you had at the shelter. Heck, my human gave me two, one for when I want to be by myself and one for when I want to be with him. He's so thoughtful!

Rule No. 7: Don't bark unless it's important. Many humans don't like yappy dogs. On the other hand, most don't do anything about it when you won't shut up, except yell at you. In other words, most of us can bark all we want and get away with it. But be a good dog, okay? Be the adult in the relationship and take responsibility for your actions. I know my human is very appreciative of my self-restraint.

Rule No. 8: It won't be easy, but you should teach your human to be consistent both in daily routines and discipline. As with the barking, many are not good at this, especially discipline. But you can do it if you're firm with your human. And as a result, life will be much more pleasant for both of you.

Rule No. 9: Your human's priorities will not always be yours, especially when you go for a walk. That's because he has a disability. He can't smell nearly as well as you, and thus misses many of finer fragrances in the outdoors you enjoy lingering over, including road kill, rotten leaves, and rabbit poop. Remarkably, he also doesn't understand the importance of frequent stops to assess the situation and then assert your scent over another dog's with an appropriately placed squirt. Be patient with him. Exercising a little self-restraint will help preserve harmony. Try to save your stops for only the most irresistible scents. And, believe me, I know that will be difficult. After four human years, I'm still struggling with this one.

On a personal note, my human has lived up to the vibe and smell I got from him when we first met. For the most part, that is. After all, he's only human, and I always try to remember that when he demands we leave a particularly savory scent too soon or when he returns home and expresses displeasure to find me snuggled in his bed. Day in and day out, we are happy together. Follow my rules and you can be too.

24. My Best Friend

We crossed the road onto Pippa's favorite place, a large area of little-used common ground where she chases squirrels up scattered oak trees and then wonders where they went. As I unleashed her, I looked up to see a medium-size brown and white dog charging at us from the other side. It probably outweighed Pippa by 20 or 30 pounds.

As she blossomed and embraced the outside world—except for thunder, gun shots, and fireworks—my speedy black companion decided that every person is a friend who wants to pet her and every animal is someone with whom to play or at least encounter in the spirit of peaceful co-existence, as evidenced by her interactions with kittens, a possum, and many other dogs.

Squirrels might be the only exception. But since she's never caught one, and likely never will despite her blinding speed, I don't know for certain.

Pippa charged right back at the brown and white dog with a bounce I've come to recognize as her happy gait. She had found a new playmate.

It skidded to a stop and ran back across the road. Pippa's enthusiasm can be intimidating to those who don't know her. But in the years since I adopted her from the shelter, I had never seen her show aggression. In fact, I wondered if she was capable of it.

*   *   *   *   *

That episode awakened a memory of what had happened with my previous companion, Ursa, who was also sweet and passive. And it made me realize maybe I should take precautions to protect Pippa when we walk, as I had been slow to do with Ursa. If the brown and white dog had attacked her, what would I have done? She would instinctively defend herself, I hoped. Or, even better, she'd run away, since she could outrun just about any attacker. But since she'd been sheltered from the world for two years and still was learning about it after nearly four, I wasn't certain.

As I walked with Ursa on a leash down a public road, a man yelled at me to step on the chain attached to a small dog running out of his yard. I obliged. He came to retrieve the dog and thanked me. We hadn't talked more than 10 seconds when his wife opened the door to their house and a large yellow Lab charged off the porch, across the yard, and attacked Ursa. Although Ursa was a fairly large dog at 75 pounds, this beast outweighed her by at least 50. And its intent was obvious: To kill her.

The woman futilely called for "Angel" to return. She was ignored as the Lab snarled and growled and attempted to gain purchase with her teeth so that she could begin ripping and tearing Ursa was on a leash and couldn't escape or maneuver. I don't know what the man was doing. I didn't care.

I kicked Angel repeatedly in the ribs with my hiking boots. As I did, I distantly heard the man yelling, "Stop! Stop!" Finally, I managed to knock Angel off Ursa, and the Lab fled, although I'm not sure where. I looked at the man incredulously.

"Are you kidding me?" I said. "Your dog was trying to kill mine and you wanted me to stop?"

He replied, "I was afraid she'd attack you."

As I checked Ursa to make that she was okay—and blessedly, she was—I said, "If she had, then *you* would have been the one with the problem."

From that point on, I started carrying a large, sturdy walking stick to protect both Ursa and me.

For the twice daily walks with Pippa, I hadn't gotten into the habit. I should have, especially after what happened late one afternoon as we walked in an unfamiliar area. As we approached some houses on a gravel road I put her on the leash, as I always do where there's a chance we'll encounter traffic or meet people and other pets.

Suddenly, two large black and white dogs, resembling border collies on steroids, appeared in a front yard to our left. They spied us and charged just as I saw them. They barked while streaking toward us and then maneuvered away from me in an attempt to get at Pippa. The smaller of the two held back a bit as the other attacked. Pippa growled in self-defense and dodged the larger dog, but her agility was limited by the leash.

With her attention diverted, the second dog closed in. In response, I kicked at it first, and then delivered a glancing blow to the more aggressive of the two. Both dogs backed off.

"Get out of here!" I yelled, and they retreated a little more, still barking and snarling. I hoped their owner would hear me and step outside to see what was going on. That didn't happen.

But I bought enough time to reach down to the road and pick up a golf-ball-size rock. Just as I stood back up, the larger dog attacked again. With about 10 feet separating us, I let fly.

Now the odds of hitting a target with a rock when it is running straight toward you aren't good. In hindsight, I realize that. During that precarious moment, though, the rock was my only option.

And, somehow, some way, that stone struck the beast squarely on the nose. It wasn't exactly a David-Goliath moment, since I outweighed the dog and it didn't fall to the ground from the blow. But it did yelp in what appeared to be agonizing pain, and continued to bawl as it ran back into the yard. The second dog kept barking, but also kept its distance as we passed.

*   *   *   *   *

As Pippa forgot the brown and white dog and bounded down the hill to find squirrels, I remembered I still had that stick in the garage and wondered whether I should start carrying it again. We'd been fortunate in our encounter with the collies. But what if that brown and white dog had been just as aggressive? How would I have defended her this time?

A friend who walks his small, brown mixed breed along the same roads told me he carries pepper spray to defend himself and his companion. That might be something worth considering too, I realized.

Although I dislike harming a dog, sometimes it's necessary, especially to protect yourself, a family member, or your own pet. But while aggressive dogs pose the danger, owners are the ones really to blame for the threat that they pose. Responsible dog owners must take into account not only breed temperament, but individual personalities and circumstances when allowing their pets around other animals or people.

For example, Angel was a Lab, a breed generally known as friendly, lovable, and harmless. But she also was an adult, and her owners had to know that she was aggressive toward other dogs, especially if she perceived they posed a danger to her family and/ or property, which she probably did. That aggression can be easily explained this way: Some, such as Angel, are alphas toward other dogs, and will either kill them or force subjugation. Others, like Pippa and Ursa, are betas, who get along fine with other members of the pack. The owner of an alpha usually can control the dog, but, sometimes, it can pose a danger to other humans, especially children, for the same reason it goes after other dogs.

Angel wasn't the first Lab to be aggressive toward Ursa. When I took her to the home of a fishing buddy, his dog snarled and growled, and had to be confined until we left. By contrast, his dog was friendly and gentle with almost all people.

Labs are a surprising eighth on the list of the 35 breeds that have attacked the most people during the past three decades, according to Graphiq's *Pet Breeds* website. Part of that can be explained by their sheer numbers, as the American Kennel Club (AKC) reports they are the most popular breed in this country. Not surprisingly, the top three breeds for attacks and fatalities are pit bull, Rottweiler, and German shepherd. Pit bulls lead by a large margin, with 3,397 attacks and 295 deaths, compared to the Rot's 535 and 85. Labs accounted for 56 attacks and 3 deaths over the last 30 years.

Additionally, *Animals 24-7* says pit bulls killed 24,000 dogs and 13,000 cats in 2015. "Most of their owners themselves are higher risk people, thus creating a recipe for a dog-bite disaster," adds the *Canine Journal*.

The AKC estimates that 4.5 million people a year are bitten by dogs in the United States. Not surprisingly, for me at least, Chihuahuas are the dogs most likely bite, followed by bulldog breeds, and then the pit bull, according to the *Puppy Lover News* website. That's from a dog population of more than 83 million in about 57 million households.

Yes, a pit bull can be gentle and loving with children, as can most any dog, but it can also be unpredictable and attack without warning. That's why so many people looking to adopt avoid them. More than 30 percent of dogs in shelters are either pure pit bulls or recognizable mixes, even though they make up just six percent of the dog population.

When I went with my friend Bob to a St. Louis shelter to check out a Lab mix he'd seen online, we were stunned to see how many animals were pit bulls or "mixes" with obvious pit bull parentage. We estimated the number at more than half. Bob decided he didn't want the Lab mix, and he wasn't interested in any of the others. I agreed with his decision about the latter.

Along the areas where Pippa and I walk, one particular German shepherd frightens me the most. It's kept in a fenced backyard, where it barks ferociously as we pass. I can understand that. The animal is protecting its territory. But occasionally I see a young man walking it on a leash. Or rather the dog is dragging him, and they aren't anywhere near their home. He has little to no control over the animal and it snarls and desperately lunges toward Pippa and me, while we stay as far away as possible.

German shepherds are among the most intelligent of dogs and they learn quickly. But they can also become over-protective of family and territory. If not socialized correctly, as in this case, they pose a danger to others.

"Truth is that any dog can and—if the conditions are right—will bite, no matter how well bred, well trained, or loved they may be. The key is being both aware of breed tendencies and general stressors, but not afraid (fear feeds aggression)," the *Canine Journal* adds.

A dog trainer once told me that even normally gentle pets will bite their owners if they are presented with a circumstance they perceive as threatening, such as suddenly viewing the owner from a peer-to-peer perspective. A man was on his hands and knees, crawling into the bathroom, to scare his wife, the trainer explained, when their dog suddenly bit him in the face.

Canine Journal offers these tips for preventing dog bites:

- Don't approach an unfamiliar animal.
- If an unfamiliar dog approaches you, remain motionless. Do not run or scream. Avoid direct eye contact.
- Don't disturb a dog while it's eating, sleeping, or taking care of its puppies.
- Allow a dog to sniff and smell you before you attempt to pet it. Afterward scratch the animal under the chin, not on the head.
- Report strays or dogs displaying strange behavior to your local animal control.
- If attacked, roll into a ball and remain motionless. Avoid eye contact and remain calm.

*   *   *   *   *

Defending against irrational and irate humans is another matter. In the 18 years that I've been walking twice a day with Ursa and then Pippa, I never encountered one until recently. Before that frightening morning, we met only friendly people who were either out working in their yards, fishing the lakes, or walking their own dogs.

This guy moved in about 1/2 mile away, on one of our alternating routes. His house sits on the edge of two acres, while the rest is open and slants downhill from a gravel road to a lake. Two isolated oaks grow at the far side, just a few yards from dense woods.

We were well past the house, but not yet beyond his property, when I unleashed Pippa so she could run down the hill and into the woods in pursuit of squirrels. We were on a little traveled road with no houses ahead for quite awhile. As always, she ran down the road, past the open ground, and into the woods. Only this time, a squirrel ran out of them and up one of the oak trees on the edge of the homeowner's property. Pippa followed, and, as she always does when she's treed a squirrel, she didn't bark or make any kind of disturbance. She stood there looking around, as if not certain what to do next.

Before I could call her to me, an angry male voice from the deck on the back of the house shouted, "Is that your dog?" Not waiting for a response, the voice added, "Get him off my property!"

Had the man given me the time, I would have apologized and promised it wouldn't happened again. But before I could, he launched into a tirade, yelling so fast and with such force that I couldn't understand much of what he said. I might have recognized a few expletives. After pausing for breath, he added, "Did you hear me?"

"No," I said honestly. It really didn't matter though. The tone clearly conveyed irrational and potentially dangerous anger. Pure and simple, this was road rage without the car.

Once again he screamed, probably repeating what he said before.

This time when he stopped, I said as loudly as I could, "Welcome to the neighborhood!" And with Pippa on her leash, I picked up the pace to quickly put the woods between his line of sight and us.

"I'm going to find out who you are!" he yelled.

Although I was in the wrong for allowing Pippa to go onto his property, his response was so irrational and threatening that I reported the incident to the police. I want a record on file if I have another encounter with him and he threatens Pippa and me with more than just four-letter words. But I don't intend to provoke him again, so I avoid walking that route with Pippa.

Happily, more new neighbors proved to be the polar opposite of that sad and angry man. As we approached their house one afternoon, they pulled into their driveway. I quickly put Pippa on the leash, as I always do when we're around people she doesn't know. They saw me and, as they exited the car, said, "Oh, you don't have to do that!"

They knelt and tried to coax her toward them to be petted. And, as Pippa always does with strangers, she ran eagerly toward them, but then backed off at the last moment and bounced around just out of range. She wanted to comply, she wanted to be petted, but her shyness, probably because of little socialization for the first two years of her life, prevented her from letting them touch her.

I explained her background, and, as pet owners who helped sustain a no-kill shelter in a nearby county, they understood. "She can come here anytime," they said. "She can go wherever she wants in our yard."

Treats for Pippa followed shortly after the first meeting, and she now eagerly runs to be petted when she sees them. Those are my kind of neighbors. Pippa's too. And when I told them, "Welcome to the neighborhood," I really meant it.

*   *   *   *   *

Considerably slower afoot than my speedy companion, I was just a few yards from where Pippa and I encountered the brown and white dog. The early spring sunshine felt good on my face as I watched her, well down the hill now, perhaps 100 yards away. She stood under an oak tree, wondering where the squirrel went.

Our morning and evening adventures usually occur that way. I walk three miles, while she runs at least six, often prancing back and forth in front of me until I catch up.

Suddenly, I heard movement and turned to see the brown and white dog rushing at me. It wasn't growling, but its ears were back and its teeth bared, making its intent obvious. It was going to attack me. Perhaps that had been its original goal until Pippa's exuberant approach startled it and forced a temporary retreat.

With no rock, no stick, and no pepper spray to defend myself, I braced for the attack, hoping to fend off the beast with a kick to the guts, or preferably the head. This was no bluff. It was going to try to tear into me.

But it never got the chance. Seemingly out of nowhere, Pippa streaked by me from behind, and, as with the brown and white dog, her ears also were back and teeth bared. Although I never had seen this gait from her before, I clearly could read it. It said, "Get the hell out of here!"

As it had the first time, my would-be attacker jolted to a halt, reversed course, and tried to run away. He didn't make it until after Pippa delivered a bite to his hindquarters, which prompted a most pleasant—for me, at least—yelp of pain.

Then, as if nothing extraordinary had just happened, Pippa trotted back to my side. She didn't even look up for approval. But I certainly did approve. I petted her, praised her, and pressed my head to hers. "Thanks," I said softly, completely at odds with an internal voice that was shrieking with wonder and amazement.

My sweet Pippa liked everyone and every animal. Until seconds ago, she had never shown an ounce of aggression for any reason. Consequently, I was worrying about how best to defend her. I never considered she was capable of defending me. After all, when she was frightened, usually by a loud noise or strangers who were a little too aggressive in trying to pet her, she came running and leaned against my leg for comfort.

But she was capable, brave, and strong, and when circumstances required it, she would be my champion, just as I would be hers. The bond we forged during our nearly four years together suddenly seemed even more remarkable, more miraculous. And the phrase "man's best friend" took on a whole new meaning for me. I gave Pippa extra treats when we got home.

ROBERT MONTGOMERY

25. Today

"Everyone thinks they have the best dog. And none of them are wrong."

— *W.R. Purche*

Pippa never will be a "normal" dog, and I'm okay with that. In fact, I'm more than okay. I love her more because of it. She survived two years in a shelter, and yet brightens my life each and every day because of her unbridled enthusiasm for life in general and her fierce determination to eventually catch a squirrel in particular.

Yes, I wish she wouldn't be so shy around people, especially friends. And I wish she would relax more instead of pacing, as she sometimes does in the house while I'm working or at my friend Bob's, when he has other guests. She's still an independent sort too, especially at night. When we come in from our afternoon/evening walk, she often stays in the basement until morning.

But more and more, she comes up during the day and hits my elbow with her long nose to request affection. And as I stroke her head or gently massage the fur of her neck, she places her paw over my forearm. Sometimes she naps on a bed I've placed between my recliner-office and a French door, so she can soak up afternoon sun. If the weather is warm enough, I'll allow her out on the deck for both rays and fresh air. She loves that. Occasionally after dark, she comes up to nose her way into some "good night" cuddling.

In the outdoors she truly shines, possibly because freedom to run and romp was denied her for so long. Unless threatening weather intervenes, her contagious enthusiasm for each morning and afternoon outing never varies. Often, as we are walking and for no apparent reason, she will take an insanity break. It might take the form of suddenly rolling in a pile of dead leaves or dead grass, moaning exquisitely as she does so. Or it might come in the form of a feint at me so I can pretend to chase her, inspiring manic laps until she's nearly exhausted.

In the outdoors she seems most loving and bonded with me. Sometimes she walks by my side, leaning on my leg, just as she did the day I first saw her at the shelter. Only now she pushes her head up against my hand so I'll pet her. Also, she looks to me for protection when she's frightened, and she's eager to protect me if I'm threatened. Outside, we are one.

If we're not on foot, Pippa loves to ride with me in the car. Of course, she's enjoyed that almost from the start. Sadly, though, her stomach didn't. But we've persevered, with me cleaning up messes and her gradually becoming acclimated to the motion of a car. Now, weather permitting, I often take her with me to run errands, go shopping, and even ride along as I deliver Meals on Wheels.

She was with me yesterday as I pulled up near an apartment to take a meal to one of my regulars, a big, burly guy with a gray ponytail. I suspect he used to ride a motorcycle, probably a Harley. He has a Chihuahua named "Baby," and we are friends. I always bring her a biscuit.

He was sitting in the shade by his front door watching me as I got out of the car, stroked Pippa on the head, and told her I'd would be right back.

As I approached him, I looked for Baby, but she wasn't there. Before I could ask, he told me. During the night, he'd gotten out of bed, tripped over the line to his oxygen tank, and fell on Baby, breaking her neck.

What can you say in response to that? Any words are inadequate. I didn't tell him I know how awful it feels to believe you've contributed to the death of a beloved companion. No, my actions didn't directly cause Ursa's death five years before, as his did Baby's. But the guilt I felt was almost unbearable, and possibly equal to his, after she fell backward down a flight of stairs as she attempted to join me on the deck. I'll never know how much, if any, that fall contributed to her death. Because of her failing health, I'd already made the tough decision to take her on one final trip to the vet the following day. But that fall certainly wasn't good for her. And the horrible image of her plunging down those stairs when she was just one step away from the top, because she wanted to be with me, will remain with me forever.

"Oh, man, I'm so sorry," I said.

I handed him his meal and walked away, wishing I could say something, anything, to ease his grief. But I didn't know him well enough, and his pain was too fresh to suggest what I thought would be best for him.

I'm sure the moment he fell on Baby will live with him the rest of his life, just as the image of Ursa's fall stays with me. And I know I wouldn't want to hear it if someone told me I should get another dog right away.

But now, as someone who did wait too long to get another dog, I can speak with some authority on the subject. Life is too short and waiting serves no purpose, other than to deny yourself happiness.

It doesn't matter if your dog died in a horrible accident as Baby did, from a degenerative disease likes Daisy, or from failing health and old age as Ursa did. Death happens. It's an evitable consequence of life.

Whether we chose dogs or dogs chose us thousands of years ago, doesn't matter. They are devoted to us, and we are happier when we share our lives with them.

Yes, Baby was special. Yes, Daisy was special. Yes, Ursa was special. And other dogs never will take their place.

But Pippa is special too, and she would be just as special if I adopted her right away instead of waiting nearly a year. That would have been one more year of happiness together. Every dog who shares your life is special. That's what they are. That's who they are.

And millions of special dogs are waiting in shelters right now for you to adopt them, so they can show you what I mean.

Appendix A

All Shelters Aren't the Same

If not for a "limited access" policy, Pippa, a remarkable, spirit-lifting companion who has enriched my life in countless ways, would have been euthanized long before we had a chance to meet.

Fortunately, that is the policy followed by the Farmington Pet Adoption Center (FPAC) in Farmington, Missouri, a no-kill facility which has found homes for thousands of dogs and cats during more than 30 years of operation.

Limited access means a shelter accepts only the number of dogs and cats it can accommodate, and no more. In the case of the FPAC, an organization supported solely by donations, that's 25 dogs and 75 cats.

"We do not euthanize for space," explained Lucretia Skaggs, a long-time FPAC board member. She added that the only time that the center euthanizes animals is for the same reasons loving owners would, because the animals are terminally ill or mortally injured.

"There's a lot of misunderstanding about what shelters do," she said. "For example, the Humane Society of Missouri is 'open intake,' which means it has to euthanize eventually."

And there's a lot of misunderstanding about how those shelters relate to their local communities and national organizations, including the Humane Society of the United States (HSUS) and the American Society for Prevention of Cruelty to Animals (ASPCA). Even though those large organizations spend big bucks on commercials soliciting donations and implying they help local shelters, little of that money filters down. "HSUS raises millions of dollars from American animal lovers through manipulative advertising, but doesn't run a single pet shelter, and isn't affiliated with any pet or local humane societies," said the *Help Pet Shelters* website.

On the other hand, state SPCAs and Humane Societies, also supported by donations, do focus on rescue, care, and adoption of animals. Municipal animal control agencies do so as well, but are much more limited because of budget constraints. They are the most likely to euthanize an animal after 30 days.

Skaggs said that FPAC staff often hears, "I pay taxes! How dare you not take this dog (or cat)!" But unlike those municipal pounds, no-kill facilities receive no taxpayer dollars. Donations are their life blood.

"There's also confusion because of our proximity to the pound," she said.

But even though pounds must euthanize because of space and budget limitations, that has been minimized in the towns around FPAC. "We're lucky," Skaggs explained. "We have a network, Farmington Rescue Friends for dogs and the Midwest Cat Alliance Community (Advocats) for cats."

These groups take photos of impounded animals and try to find places for them at other no-kill shelters and through rescue groups. FPAC does the same. Sometimes, "foster parents" help with overflow.

"We have a 90 percent no-kill rate in the community," she said. "But we can't take them all. We're always full."

And being at capacity contributes to an emotionally charged environment. "Our staff tolerates a lot," Skaggs continued, explaining that much of the angst relates to seeing neglected, abandoned, and mistreated animals.

And then there's the human element. "It's challenging to remain civil to some people," she said. "They come in and give the most asinine reasons for giving up their pets, like getting new furniture."

Bottom line, if you really want to contribute to the welfare of animals, give locally to private no-kill shelters like FPAC, to breed rescue groups, or to local animal control agencies.

Here's a look at how the FPAC operates:

With an annual budget of $225,000, it depends solely on financial donations or merchandise donations such as clothing and household items for its resale store. The store provides about 60 percent of the center's revenue, which roughly covers staffing costs. A few fundraisers help as well.

"Without the store, we couldn't function," Skaggs said.

The shelter typically has four full-time employees and six part-time. "We used paid workers to care for the animals because they're trained and more reliable to keep to a schedule," she explained.

About 20 to 25 volunteers, including board members, also help out. Much of that effort goes toward maintaining and operating the store.

Next to staffing, veterinarian bills are the second highest cost, and utilities come third. Fortunately, vets typically charge a reduced rate to care for shelter animals.

FPAC buys most of its food, occasionally receiving donations. "But with donations, you don't get consistent product," Skaggs said. "We buy food with no corn, gluten, or soy.

"Our most pressing needs are money and good quality clothing and household items for the store," she added.

The most rewarding aspect of donating time and effort to a no-kill shelter "is finding the perfect home for a pet," she said. "You see a person walk in that door and make that connection. You see the beginnings of that bond forming.

"This is the most heartbreaking and heartwarming thing I've ever done."

Puppies for Parole

In addition to obtaining a dog that's already spayed or neutered, when you adopt from FPAC or other shelters in Missouri, you just might get one already trained. That's because of Puppies for Parole, a program run through the Missouri Department of Corrections. Other states have similar projects, though with different names.

Here's what the MDOC says about the eight-week program:

"Puppies for Parole is a unique program made possible through our partnerships with animal shelters and animal advocate groups statewide. Selected offenders have the opportunity to become trainers to rescue dogs in the program. Offenders work with the dogs, teaching them basic obedience skills and properly socializing the animals, making them more adoptable. Once the dogs have successfully completed the program, they will be adopted through their original shelters.

"There are multiple benefits to this program. Puppies for Parole gives offenders the skills necessary to support successful rehabilitation and reentry, ultimately improving public safety. At the same time, this is an opportunity for the offenders to repay

Missouri communities and repair some of the debts caused by their crimes. We have seen this program have a profound effect on the inmates and staff, increasing the safety and security of the facility.

"The program also saves dogs' lives. Many dogs that were unwanted and would have been euthanized have found forever homes through the program. More than 4,000 dogs have graduated from the program and been adopted. Some of these dogs were specially trained to work with the disabled, special needs children, veterans and mental health patients.

"Finally, Puppies for Parole uses no general revenue and operates solely on private donations and donations from offender organizations."

Appendix B

Why You Should Adopt

You'll Save a Life

Sadly, between three and four million dogs and cats are euthanized each year in the United States simply because too many people give up their pets and too few people adopt from shelters. Because of limited space at shelters, staff members must sometimes make difficult decisions to euthanize animals that haven't been adopted. The number of euthanized animals could be reduced dramatically if more people adopted pets instead of buying them. By adopting from a private humane society or animal shelter, a breed rescue group, or a local animal control agency, you'll help save the lives of two animals—the pet you adopt and a homeless animal somewhere that can be rescued because of space you helped free up.

You'll Get a Healthy Pet

Animal shelters are brimming with happy, healthy animals just waiting for someone to take them home. Most shelters examine and give vaccinations to animals when they arrive, and many spay or neuter them before adoption. In addition to medical care, more and more shelters also screen animals for specific temperaments and behaviors to make sure each family finds the right pet for its lifestyle.

It's a common misconception that animals end up in shelters because they've been abused or done something "wrong." In fact, most animals are given to shelters because of "people reasons," not because of anything they've done. Things like a divorce, a move, lack of time, or financial constraints are among the most common reasons pets lose their homes.

You'll Save Money

Adopting a pet from an animal shelter is much less expensive than buying a pet from a pet store or through other sources. In addition, animals from many shelters are already spayed or neutered and vaccinated, which makes the shelter's fee a real bargain.

You'll Feel Better

Pets have a way of putting a smile on your face and a spring in your step. Not only do animals give you unconditional love, they are psychologically, emotionally, and physically beneficial. For all age groups, caring for a companion animal can provide a sense of purpose and fulfillment and lessen feelings of loneliness and isolation.

Pets can help your physical health as well. Just spending time with an animal can lower your blood pressure and cholesterol levels, and dog walking, pet grooming, and even petting provide increased physical activity that can help strengthen the heart, improve blood circulation, and slow the loss of bone tissue. Put simply, pets are more than good friends. They're also good medicine and can improve a person's well-being in many ways.

You Won't Be Supporting Puppy Mills and Pet Stores

Puppy mills are "factory style" dog-breeding facilities that put profit above the welfare of dogs. Most dogs raised in puppy mills are housed in shockingly poor conditions with improper medical care, and the parents of the puppies are kept in cages to be bred over and over for years, without human companionship and with little hope of ever joining a family. And after they're no longer profitable, breeding dogs are simply discarded—either killed, abandoned, or sold at auction.

Puppy mill puppies are sold to unsuspecting consumers in pet stores, over the Internet, and through newspaper classified advertisements to whoever is willing to pay for them. They are marketed as coming from great breeders, with well-rehearsed sales tactics to keep money flowing to the puppy mill, while ensuring buyers never get to see where the pups actually come from. Many of the puppies have serious behavioral and health problems that might not be apparent for months, including medical issues that can cost thousands of dollars to treat, if they're treatable at all. Unfortunately, many people are not even aware puppy mills exist, so when they buy a pet from a pet store, online or other retail outlet, they unwittingly support this cruel industry.

By adopting instead of buying a pet, you can be certain you aren't supporting cruel puppy mills with your money. Puppy mills will continue to operate until people stop purchasing their dogs. Instead of buying a dog, visit your local shelter where you will probably find dozens of healthy, well-socialized puppies and adult dogs—including purebreds—just waiting for that special home: yours.

(From Farmington Pet Adoption Center)

Acknowledgements

*M*ostly supported by donations and volunteers, no-kill pet shelters like the Farmington Pet Adoption Center, do wonderful work that often is unrecognized, unappreciated, and misunderstood. A special thanks to the FPAC, where Pippa was cared for until fate brought us together there in 2013, and to board member Lucretia Skaggs. And words are inadequate to express the gratitude I feel for the kindness of Billy, Damien, and Sarah Bell, who rescued and returned Pippa to me.

About the Author

R obert U. Montgomery and Pippa live in the eastern Ozarks, where they'd rather be outdoors. During four years together, they have walked more than 4,000 miles.

Montgomery is the author of four other books, including *Under the Bed: Tales from an Innocent Childhood; Fish, Frogs, and Fireflies: Growing Up with Nature,* and *Why We Fish: Reel Wisdom from Real Fishermen* from NorLights Press and *Better Bass Fishing* from Countryman Press.

He also is the founder of the *Activist Angler,* a website devoted to promoting and protecting recreational fishing, and a Senior Writer for B.A.S.S. Publications, specializing in conservation and environmental issues. In addition, the Missouri native is winner of the prestigious Homer Circle Fishing Communicator Award. He has fished and photographed wildlife in Africa, South America, and Central America, as well as North America.

Made in the USA
Monee, IL
11 November 2023